The Bournemouth & Poole College

250221102 F

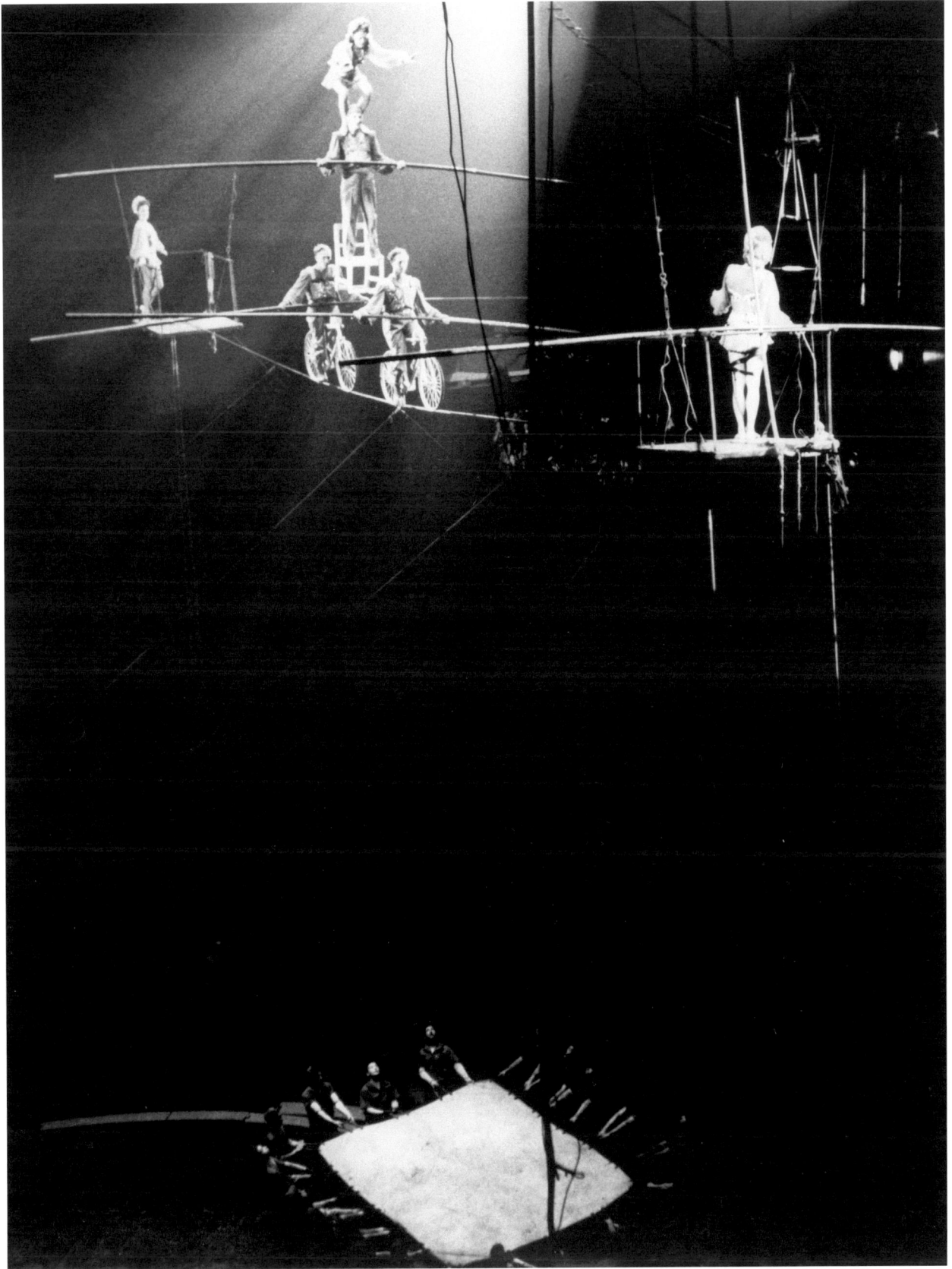

"Mama's in the Park" costume design

Miles White (1914–2000)
1955
Paint and pencil on paper
12 × 10 in. (30.5 × 25.4 cm)
The John and Mable Ringling Museum of Art, Tibbals Collection, ht300748

When John Ringling North brought in new talent to liven up the show during the 1940s, perhaps his most important hire was Miles White (1914–2000), a designer who had worked in the studio of Norman Bel Geddes. White had done most of the work on the "Old King Cole" spec in 1941, and from 1942 through 1955 he was primary costume and production designer for the Ringling Bros. and Barnum & Bailey Circus. White was joined by the Broadway director John Murray Anderson in 1942, and the two employed a concept that transformed the circus into something that more resembled a theatrical extravaganza. He was an instrumental figure in modernizing the look of the show and worked to highlight the artistry of the performers with his designs. During this time, the circus settled into staging four new production numbers each season, which usually consisted of an entrée, an aerial routine, an animal routine, and the finale.

For the 1955 season, the circus mounted some of the most lavish spectacle numbers in its history, all inventively costumed by White. This included a spec called "Mamas in the Park," which featured adult elephants pushing baby elephants in bonnets around the track in oversized carriages, accompanied by dozens of cancan dancers with the clowns as Keystone Kops and Emmett Kelly in the role of a park bum. White's design for the dancers was an elegant dress in alternating colors with a feathered headdress and small parasol as accessories. The elaborate costumes were his last for the circus, as cost-cutting measures led to his being let go before the following season. While working for the Ringling Bros. and Barnum & Bailey Circus, White also continued to design for Broadway and Hollywood, winning Tony Awards for Best Costume Design (1951 and 1953), and earning three Oscar nominations (1952, 1954, and 1956). Miles White was a transcendent talent who had an immeasurable impact on the look and feel of the circus, and it was hardly an accident that his time with the show coincided with one of the most successful stretches in the show's history.

Fig. 31A. Sverre O. Braathen. Pat Lombardo and unknown woman in "Mama's in the Park" spectacle wardrobe. July 8, 1955. Kodachrome. Illinois State University's Special Collections, Milner Library, Normal, Illinois, BSP2995.

References: "New Shine for the Circus," *Life* (June 20, 1955), 79–84; Albrecht, "Miles White"; Pecktal, *Costume Design*, 226–39; Monsos, "Miles White."

M-6

"New Madison Square Garden—Season 1926—Ringling Brothers and Barnum & Bailey Concert Band.—Merle Evans, Band Master."

Edward J. Kelty (1888–1967)
1926
Gelatin silver print
12 × 20 in. (30.5 × 50.8 cm)
The John and Mable Ringling Museum of Art, Tibbals Collection, ht0004850

Circus Time

Ringling Bros and Barnum & Bailey Circus Band: Merle Evans, Conductor
1953
Vinyl LP record
Decca Records
10⅝ × 10½ in. (27 × 26.7 cm)
Shelburne Museum, Shelburne, Vermont

In terms of longevity and verve, no performer matched the career of the musician and bandmaster Merle Evans (1894–1987), who joined the combined Ringling Bros. and Barnum & Bailey Circus for its debut season. Evans was born in Columbus, Kansas, and took to the piano and cornet at a young age. By the time he was fifteen, the self-taught Evans was playing in small local bands, and he began working with an assortment of touring shows, including a season with the Buffalo Bill–101 Ranch Wild West Show. In 1919, Evans received an offer from Charles Ringling to serve as bandleader for the new combined show at a salary of $60 a week. That first season, Evans engaged thirty-one musicians for the band, and they had just one week of practice leading up to the show's debut at Madison Square Garden. Other than some union-related and family issues that took him away from the show on occasion, Evans led the band on the Ringling Bros. and Barnum & Bailey Circus for the next fifty years and retired at the end of the 1969 season.

During a typical performance, the band played more than 200 different pieces drawn from a wide variety of sources—popular tunes of the day, classical selections, and an assortment of waltzes, marches, and galops. Circus music set the mood for the performances and tied the disparate elements of the show together. It also served a more programmatic function by cueing acts and providing a rhythm for both the human and animal performers. Although Evans stood in front of the band to conduct, he also remained dedicated to playing the cornet, and he could often be seen conducting with his left hand while playing the instrument with his right. Later in his career, Evans was acclaimed as the "Toscanini of the Big Top," after the famous Italian conductor, though his musicians were not always of a similar caliber. Writing of the Evans–led band in 1923, a *New York Times* reviewer remarked that while it was "not the acme of harmony," the band made up for it with its "volume and enthusiasm." Though the quality of the music might have varied, one constant was the sartorial splendor of the band as the musicians were attired in bright new uniforms every year. From his perch in the Madison Square Garden bandstand, Merle Evans saw the rise and decline of the circus in New York City over the course of the twentieth century and provided the soundtrack to a half-century of circus spectacle.

References: "Whole Circus Run By Big Bass Drum," *New York Times*, April 11, 1923; "Spotlight Passes Maestro of Circus," *New York Times*, April 13, 1941; Plowden, *Merle Evans*.

NEW MADISON SQUARE GARDEN—SEASON 1926—RINGLING BROTHERS AND BARNUM & BAILEY CONCERT BAND.—MERLE EVANS, BAND MASTER.

"And the show! What gifted pen shall describe it? Where is the word painter that can portray its composite impression? Taken as a whole it cannot be pictured. To dissect and coldly catalogue it piece by piece seems almost sacrilege."
—*Billboard,* 1903

CIRCUS
and the City

New York, 1793–2010

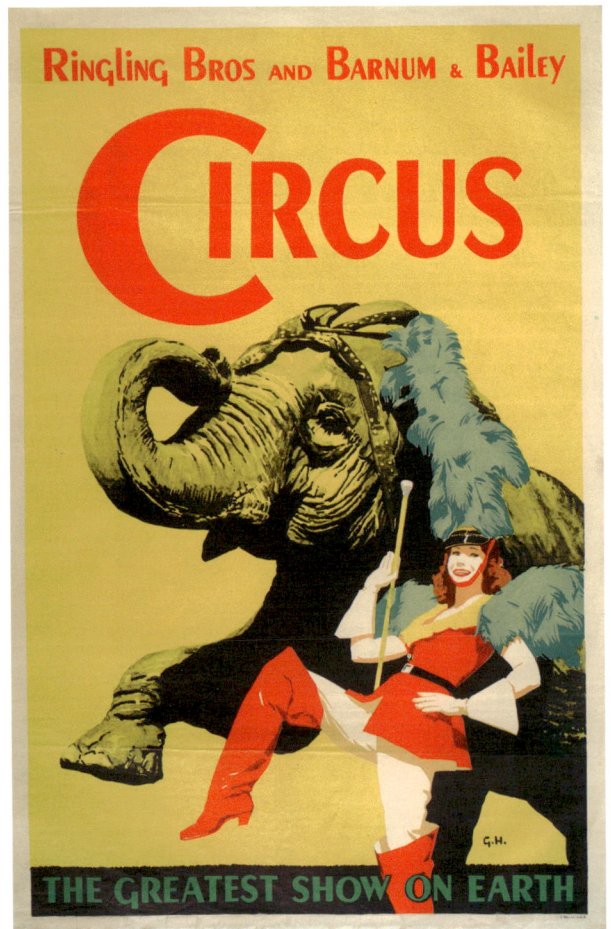

27

Sleeping at the circus, Madison Square Garden, New York
Weegee (1899–1968)
June 28, 1943
Gelatin silver print
10 ⅜ × 13 ⅝ in. (26.4 × 34.6 cm)
International Center of Photography, New York,
Bequest of Wilma Wilcox, 1993 (2367.1993)

"'Spangles,' the new Ringling Brothers Continental Circus, has the dazzling aerial acts of the old show, as these upturned faces in the audience testify."
Weegee (1899–1968)
June 18, 1943
Gelatin silver print
10 ⅝ × 12 ½ in. (27 × 31.8 cm)
International Center of Photography, New York,
Bequest of Wilma Wilcox, 1993 (7959.1993)

"Resourceful girl manages to watch a man on flying trapeze and feed hot dog to escort at same time."
Weegee (1899–1968)
April 18, 1943
Gelatin silver print
7 ¾ × 9 ⅝ in. (19.7 × 24.4 cm)
International Center of Photography, New York,
Bequest of Wilma Wilcox, 1993 (7921.1993)

Circus audience, New York
Weegee (1899–1968)
ca. 1943
Gelatin silver print
9 ¼ × 7 ½ in. (23.5 × 19.1 cm)
International Center of Photography, New York,
Bequest of Wilma Wilcox, 1993 (7979.1993)

Arthur Fellig (1899–1968), better known by his pseudonym Weegee, was a photographer and photojournalist famed for his stark pictures of New York City during the 1930s and 1940s. Weegee was a Polish immigrant who is perhaps best remembered for his crime scene photography and the 1945 collection *Naked City*, which brought his work national recognition. Less well known was Weegee's fascination with the circus, which was a subject that he returned to repeatedly as he seems to have invariably visited the Ringling Bros. and Barnum & Bailey Circus during its annual stand at Madison Square Garden.

Although Weegee took some photographs of the performances and many more of clowns and staff backstage, the images used in this exhibition are drawn from a series of pictures that he made of the audience, an underexplored subject in circus historiography. In the early 1940s, he turned his camera to focus on the range of emotions experienced by spectators at Madison Square Garden. Dissatisfied by his inability to capture candid images, Weegee on at least one occasion played the role of a clown in the show and used an enormous prop camera to disguise his real one, so that he could take pictures without tipping off his subjects. Most of the photographs in this series were taken in 1943, the same year Weegee went "undercover" at the short-lived Spangles summer circus at Madison Square Garden, although it is difficult to tell precisely which photographs were taken surreptitiously. The photographs portray New York in all its diversity—children, women, businessmen, men and women in uniform, an African-American couple—and show the range of responses, from laughter to wonder to apprehension, inspired by the spectacular circus acts.

References: "Weegee, as Clown"; Lee and Meyer, *Weegee and Naked City*; Barth, *Weegee's World*.

"Ringling Bros and Barnum & Bailey Circus / The Greatest Show on Earth" with Felix Adler

George Howe (1886–1955)
1943
Color lithograph poster
McCandlish Lithograph Corp., Philadelphia
21 × 28 in. (53.3 × 71.1 cm)
The John and Mable Ringling Museum of Art, Tibbals Collection, ht2001715

Felix Adler clown shoes

ca. 1950
Leather
19 × 10 × 10 in. (48.3 × 25.4 × 25.4 cm)
Circus World Museum, CWi-2653

Some of the biggest stars of the Ringling Bros. and Barnum & Bailey Circus during the twentieth century were the clowns Otto Griebling, Emmett Kelly, Lou Jacobs, and Felix Adler. Griebling and Kelly were famous for their work as tramp clowns, and Adler and Jacobs developed their own unique styles. Felix Adler (1895–1960) was born on a farm in Iowa to a family of Jewish immigrants, and by the age of thirteen he was working for a circus. He eventually joined the Ringling Bros. show as a full-time employee in a variety of different capacities before he took to clowning. Adler honed his craft for several years before settling on his "look," which was grotesque whiteface with a large red nose into which he embedded the appropriate birthstone each month. But his most distinctive feature was an inflated suit that gave him a giant rear end. Adler also employed a number of props, including a humorous birdcage hat, and, most famously, a tiny umbrella. He was best known for his acts that involved trained piglets, who walked on their hind legs or went down a slide in exchange for a bottle of milk. In the most famous of these acts, Adler pretended to be the Big Bad Wolf, outfitted with an oversized coat and a tiny umbrella, while three piglets chased him around the ring.

Adler had a very clear philosophy of clowning: "The clown's humor is based on two things. The first is doing something that looks serious, but turns out to be funny. . . . There is a very narrow dividing line between comedy and tragedy, and the clown finds it. The second essential for him is surprise; the unexpected makes the people laugh." In fact, in some of his most talked-about acts, the endings were often a surprise, even to him. One such incident, reported by the *New York Times*, occurred when Adler was leading a mule in overshoes around the ring. The mule was trained to balk while Adler pushed futilely from behind, but "on this particular afternoon, when Adler pushed from behind, the mule unexpectedly reared. The clown slipped and fell, and the mule promptly fell in his lap." Although the audience was delighted, Adler ruefully recalled that "but of course, not for love, oats or sugar could I ever get that mule to sit in my lap again."

Other than a few years when he was off the show because of internal power struggles and union disputes, he stayed with the Ringling Bros. and Barnum & Bailey Circus for almost fifty years. At his death, John Ringling North was quoted in *Billboard*, saying that "it will be hard for us circus veterans to adjust to the sight of the clown parade without Felix and his baby pig." It was certainly true that Adler and his pigs had touched the lives of many, for not only had audiences seen his shows, but some had even provided adoptive homes for his pigs once they were too old to perform, providing a tangible link between the "King of Clowns" and his fans.

Fig. 28A. Sverre O. Braathen. "Felix Adler of Clinton, Illinois a very good clown in a close-up view. July 28, 1948." Kodachrome slide. Illinois State University's Special Collections, Normal, Illinois, Milner Library, BSP1291.

References: "33 Years a Clown, He's a Circus Fan Yet," *New York Times*, April 17, 1949; "Felix Adler Dies; Clowned Half Century," *Billboard*, February 8, 1960, 47; Swortzell, *Here Come the Clowns*, 222; Speaight, *The Book of Clowns*, 112–13; Culhane, *The American Circus*, 254.

"Hagenbeck-Wallace Trained Wild Animal Circus / Clyde Beatty the Jungle King in a Single-Handed Battle with 40 of the Most Ferocious Brutes that Breathe!"

ca. 1934
Color lithograph poster
Erie Lithograph & Printing Company, Erie, Penn.
20¼ × 28 in. (51.4 × 71.1 cm)
The John and Mable Ringling Museum of Art,
Tibbals Collection, ht2000830

Clyde Beatty pith helmet

ca. 1940
Pith
Label: "Genuine Pith Helmet made in India expressly for Bailey of California"
13½ × 10¼ × 7 in. (34.3 × 26.1 × 17.8 cm)
Circus World Museum, CWi-2643

Clyde Beatty whip

ca. 1940
Leather
11¾ × 15 × 1 in. (29.9 × 38.1 × 2.6 cm)
Circus World Museum, CWi-2650

One of the most sensational circus stars of the twentieth century was Clyde Beatty (1903–1965), a handsome and charismatic wild-animal trainer who took the country by storm in the 1930s. Born in Bainbridge, Ohio, in 1903, Beatty joined his first circus as a cage boy in 1921 and was eventually apprenticed to Peter Taylor, who worked a fighting-style big cat act with the Hagenbeck–Wallace Circus. After Taylor suffered a nervous breakdown in 1925, the youthful Beatty stepped in. Echoing Isaac Van Amburgh a century earlier, Beatty was known for his "all-American fighting act" and appeared in the cage wearing a safari uniform, complete with pith helmet, white breeches, a shirt, and a pistol strapped to his waist, and carrying a whip and a chair.

By 1930 Beatty's star was on the rise as he worked with thirty-two lions and tigers in a single large cage, an impressive and dangerous feat; the following year he opened with the Ringling Bros. and Barnum & Bailey Circus in New York and Boston. John Ringling had decided to drop wild-animal acts some years earlier, but the Depression demanded star attractions, and press agent Dexter Fellows relentlessly hyped Beatty in the local and national media in the lead up to the 1931 season. Beatty debuted in Madison Square Garden on April 2, performing in the cage with a mixed group of forty lions and tigers. *Variety* praised him as "steely nerved, spectacular, well appearing and above all, a showman," but the *New York Times* was distinctly less impressed, complaining that the lion yawned during a supposedly dramatic stare down from Beatty, and the newspaper later printed a letter complaining about the way he violently clubbed the animals.

While rehearsing the following winter, Beatty was pinned and seriously bitten by his favorite lion, Nero. Although he almost died from the subsequent infection, Beatty recovered in time to open at Madison Square Garden again in 1932, and he even included Nero in the act, explaining to the press that lions, "like lightning, never strike twice." Beatty played the first few New York weeks with the "Big Show" for the next three years, but disputes with management and a successful movie career led him to strike out on his own. In 1935 he joined with Jess Adkins and Zack Terrell to form the Cole Brothers–Clyde Beatty Circus, which opened unsuccessfully opposite the Ringling Bros. and Barnum & Bailey Circus in 1937 at the New York Hippodrome. Beatty performed in New York City only on a few occasions, but his popularity ensured that wild-animal acts remained a prominent part of the American circus.

References: "Ringling–B. & B. Circus," *Variety*, April 8, 1931; "Circus Opens Here, Glorifying Lions," *New York Times*, April 4, 1931; "A Circus Act Denounced," *New York Times*, April 23, 1931; "Circus Opens Here to Song of Spring," *New York Times*, April 9, 1932; Beatty and Wilson, *Jungle Performers*, 92–93; Joys, *The Wild Animal Trainer in America*; Culhane, *The American Circus*, 208–11.

30

The Wallendas, New York
Lisette Model (1901–1983)
1945
Gelatin silver print on board
23¾ × 19 in. (60.3 × 48.3 cm)
International Center of Photography, Gift of Lisette Model Foundation
in memory of Joseph G. Blum, 1993 (106.1993)

The Flying Wallendas, as they came to be known, were a troupe of high-wire performers led by Karl Wallenda (1905–1978), who made a sensational debut at Madison Square Garden in 1928 with the Ringling Bros. and Barnum & Bailey Circus. Karl was born into a traditional German circus family, and he began performing while his stepfather was away serving in the army during World War I. From modest beginnings in beer gardens and dance halls, Wallenda eventually worked up to performing with traveling European circuses, along with his brother Herman, Joseph Geiger, and Helen Kries. When John Ringling saw their act in Cuba, he immediately booked them, and for the opening show, on April 5, 1928, the group performed its high-wire act without a safety net below, astonishing the audience. The *New York Times* reported that they "provided the real, old-time thrill, keeping the eyes of the crowd riveted on their breath-taking achievements on a tight rope strung so high in the air." At this performance they showcased the first of their two major achievements in high-wire acts—the three-high vertical pyramid, in which Joe and Herman walked across the wire while Karl balanced on a shoulder bar between them carrying Helen on his shoulders.

The Wallendas returned to Europe in the early 1930s but came back to the Ringling Brothers and Barnum & Bailey Circus for the 1934 season. This time they introduced their newest achievement, which involved riding bicycles across the wire in a variety of different configurations. It was about this time, legend has it, that a reporter who witnessed an accident wrote that they "fell so gracefully that it seemed as if they were flying," and the group was thereafter billed as the Flying Wallendas. In 1943 the *New York Times* marveled that "even the veteran patron gasped at the dome-high feats of the renowned Wallendas. . . . Not content to walk across the tight wire singly, they balanced bicycles, climbed atop them, placed a chair on a bar separating two bicycles while one Wallenda climbed atop the chair and balanced himself." It was this daring act that the Austrian–born photographer Lisette Model captured on film at Madison Square Garden, as one of the troupe members precariously balanced on the shoulders of another with only a small square of canvas held by roustabouts for protection some sixty feet below.

The fear that the audience felt for the Wallendas was justified, for the following year, while attempting to debut a double back flip, Karl lost his balance and fell, but dramatically managed to grab the wire with one hand. Not surprisingly, given the danger and difficulty of their acts, this was not the only fall that the Wallendas suffered during their years of performing. Despite these accidents, however, they kept performing their high-wire act, and Karl himself continued doing stunts until the age of 73, when he fell to his death while walking across a wire stretched between the towers of the Condado Plaza Hotel in Puerto Rico.

References: "Sea Elephant Wins Children at the Circus," *New York Times,* April 6, 1928; "14,212 Roar Welcome As Circus Opens in Garden," *New York Times,* April 10, 1943; "Wallenda Dangles after Slip at Circus," *New York Times*, May 11, 1944; Morris, *Wallenda*; "Wallenda is Killed in Fall from Wire," *New York Times,* March 23, 1978; Parkinson, "A Legend is Born."

CIRCUS
and the City

New York, 1793–2010

Matthew Wittmann

Published by the Bard Graduate Center: Decorative Arts, Design History, Material Culture, New York; and Yale University Press, New Haven and London

This catalogue is published in conjunction with the exhibition *Circus and the City*, held at the Bard Graduate Center: Decorative Arts, Design History, Material Culture from September 21, 2012, through February 3, 2013.

Curator of the Exhibition: Matthew Wittmann

Project Coordinators: Olga Valle Tetkowski and Ann Marguerite Tartsinis
Coordinator of Catalogue Photography: Alexis Mucha
Copy Editor: Barbara Burn
Catalogue Design: Laura Grey with Ben Tuttle
Printed and Bound: GHP, West Haven, Connecticut

Chief Curator and Executive Editor of
Exhibition Publications, Bard Graduate Center:
Nina Stritzler-Levine

Copyright © 2012 Bard Graduate Center: Decorative Arts, Design History, Material Culture. Copyright for the essay is held by the author and the Bard Graduate Center: Decorative Arts, Design History, Material Culture. All rights reserved. This book may not be reproduced in whole or in part, in any form (beyond that copying permitted in Sections 107 and 108 of the U.S. Copyright Law and except by reviewers for the public press), without written permission from the publisher.

Library of Congress Cataloging-in-Publication Data:
Wittmann, Matthew.
Circus and the city : New York, 1793-2010 / Matthew Wittmann.
    p. cm.
Includes bibliographical references and index.
ISBN 978-0-300-18747-2 (pbk.)
1. Circus—New York (State)—New York—History. 2.
Circus—New York (State)—New York—History—Pictorial works. I. Title.
GV1803.W58 2012
791.309747'1—dc23
                                2012020207
ISBN: 978-0-300-18747-2

Front and back cover: Jacob Harris. A policeman directs a parade of elephants from the Ringling Bros. and Barnum & Bailey Circus across the intersection of Fifth Avenue and Fifty-seventh Street in New York, March 27, 1955. Photograph. AP Photo / Jacob Harris.

Endpapers: "The Association's Celebrated and Extensive Menagerie and Aviary from the Zoological Institute in the City of New-York," 1835. Poster with woodblock illustrations. Printed by Jared W. Bell, New York. © Shelburne Museum, Shelburne, Vermont, Gift of Harry T. Peters Sr. Family, 1959, 1959-67. Chk. 12.

Frontispiece: Libsohn–Ehrenberg. "April Manhattan." *Cue, the Weekly Magazine of New York Life* (April 1945), 16.

Section dividers: Chas. Parsons. "Van Amburgh & Cos. Tuba-Rheda," ca. 1865. Color lithograph poster, printed by G. W. Endicott, New York. New York State Museum, Albany, H-1985.34.3. Chk. 63.

"Exterior View of the Grand Pavilion of Franconi's Hippodrome, Covering an Area of Two Acres, as it Appears When Erected for Public Exhibition," 1853. Tinted lithograph, printed by Sarony & Major, New York. Courtesy American Antiquarian Society. Chk. 43.

Detail of "Exterior View of Our Great City of Tents…, Literal Scenes Taken from a Photograph of the 3 Rings, Racing Track & Interior View of the 7 United Monster Shows," 1882. Color lithograph poster, printed by the Strobridge Lithographing Co., Cincinnati & New York. Somers Historical Society, Somers, New York, Hugh Grant Rowell Collection, 73.16.225. Chk. 70.

Weegee. *Spectators*, ca. 1953. Gelatin silver print. International Center of Photography, New York, Bequest of Wilma Wilcox, 1993 (8028.1993). Chk. 169.

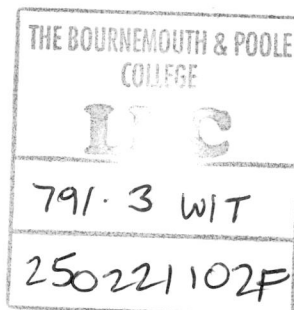

THE BOURNEMOUTH & POOLE COLLEGE

791. 3 WIT

250221102F

LCH HE
BW 9/1/14
£25-00

Circus and the City is made possible in part with support from the Mr. and Mrs. Raymond J. Horowitz Foundation for the Arts and anonymous donors.

Birdcage hat worn by
Felix Adler, ca. 1950.
Mixed media. Circus
World Museum, Baraboo,
Wisconsin, CWi-2647.
Chk. 208.

Contents

Introduction

The impetus for this project exploring the extraordinary history of the American circus came from the founder and director of the Bard Graduate Center, Susan Weber. In the course of working with the Shelburne Museum on a 2008 exhibition, *Shaker Design: Out of this World*, she was introduced to that institution's wonderful collection of circus materials. Intrigued by what she had seen at Shelburne and encouraged by the general lack of serious consideration given to the rich history of the circus in the United States, the Bard Graduate Center began to develop a project that sought to engage both an academic and a wider public audience. The initial idea for the exhibition centered on the Americanization of the circus, that is, on showing how it developed from comparatively modest European roots into the massive railroad shows that traveled around the United States during the late nineteenth and early twentieth centuries, when the circus was at the peak of its power.[1]

Such was the state of the project when I arrived at the Bard Graduate Center, and as I quickly learned, it was an idea rich in both challenges and possibilities. One major obstacle was the dearth of objects documenting the first 150 years of the American circus, beyond the relatively large amount of circus "paper," as posters and the myriad forms of print advertising were colloquially known. Wardrobe and other properties—tents, wagons, props—were used until they wore out and were either sold or recycled by shows that always had an eye on their bottom line. Moreover, the predominantly itinerant mode adopted by circuses in the United States mitigated against the accumulation of artifacts and collections. Perhaps the biggest issue,

however, was not the ephemeral nature of the circus, but the simple fact that until well into the twentieth century, many institutions did not see it as something worth documenting or preserving. Outside of the John and Mable Ringling Museum of Art in Sarasota, Florida, and the Circus World Museum in Baraboo, Wisconsin, major institutional collections are few and far between, although there are several significant archival and print-based collections housed in various libraries and museums around the United States.

The availability of materials was one concern; another challenge was simply deciding what part of the multifaceted and lengthy history of the circus in the United States to focus on. The Americanization of the circus was an important historical development, but it was not necessarily a compelling theme for an exhibition, and a number of other angles were considered and eventually discarded. At something of an impasse, I fortuitously joined hundreds of other New Yorkers (and a few protestors) on a rainy evening in March 2010 near the entrance of the Midtown Tunnel to watch the elephants of the Ringling Bros. and Barnum & Bailey Circus make their way into the city for the show's traditional spring dates at Madison Square Garden. The oddly captivating spectacle of these lumbering giants on the streets of Manhattan recalled the striking circus parades of times past and inspired me to reflect on the longer history of the circus in New York City. In a promotional stunt organized by showman P. T. Barnum over a century earlier, twenty-one elephants from the Barnum and London Circus, led by the famed Jumbo, crossed the recently completed Brooklyn Bridge as crowds thronged

"Nixon & Cos. Mammoth Circus / The Great Australian Rider James Melville as He Appeared Before the Press of New York in His Opening Rehearsal at Niblo's Garden," 1859. Tinted lithograph, printed by Sarony, Major & Knapp, New York. Courtesy American Antiquarian Society, Worcester, Massachusetts. Chk. 60.

and cheered their passage.[2] The first elephant in America had arrived in New York Harbor in 1796, some ninety years before Barnum's parade, and it was exhibited a few blocks away from the amphitheater on Broadway where the equestrian John Bill Ricketts was performing, having recently introduced the circus to the United States from Britain. Although the traditional understanding of the American circus for most people nowadays is of an enormous traveling show parading around the country with clowns, elephants, and trapeze artists performing for crowds in canvas tents, what I began to consider that evening was how the story of the circus in New York City might offer a different perspective on the historical development of this iconic form of American popular entertainment.

The theatrical, literary, and musical history of New York City are all well-traveled topics, but I soon discovered that the history of the circus—beyond P. T. Barnum, of course—had largely been overlooked by the city's cultural historians.[3] Exhibitions about the circus and the city were also few and far between,[4] and yet it seemed to be a fruitful subject, one that prompted many compelling questions. What role did the American circus play in New York City's evolution into a national and eventually a world capital of culture and entertainment? How did New York City in turn influence the dynamics and development of the circus in the United States? How was the commercialism and syncretism of the American circus intertwined with the rampant capitalism, spectacular growth, and diversity that were the defining features of the city? This approach seemed to offer a promising alternative to the typical history of the circus, one that took advantage of local collections and highlighted an overlooked aspect of the city's history.

New York is a city of superlatives, where the biggest and the best are the norm, and if any cultural form mirrored the city's energy, size, and diversity, it was the circus. But the circus was far more than simply a mirror; it also shaped life in the city, most notably in terms of popular entertainment, but also through its influence on media and advertising, in the complicated ways it intersected with the city's ongoing struggles with race,

immigration, and other social and political issues, and in the economic impact the circus had on the assorted local industries to which it was connected. Despite its ostensible timelessness, the circus is a particularly complex cultural form, one that demands a variety of different tools to unpack. It is at once a form of artistic expression and a form of commercial entertainment, one that was and is structured by a larger matrix of sociocultural institutions and economic imperatives.[5] Scholars have accordingly approached the circus from a variety of angles, from viewing the circus as a "way to understand ideological processes" to analyzing its cultural meaning using semiotics.[6] The essay that follows necessarily adopts a flexible approach to the dynamic history of the American circus, but one grounded in an understanding of the circus as something that both reflected and shaped the culture and society in which it flourished.

The essay that follows uses New York City as a lens through which to explore the development of the circus in the United States and follows a historical trajectory that echoes the structure of the exhibition. Part I, *The Early Years*, begins with Ricketts's inaugural season in 1793 and traces how the circus became part of the city's cultural fabric, developing from an essentially equestrian entertainment to a multi-act exhibition with clowns, animals, and acrobats. Part II, *The American Circus Comes of Age*, covers the burgeoning of commercial entertainment in the city from 1830 to 1870, when a recognizably American form of the circus developed and led to the formation of ever larger and more spectacular combinations. New York City's various media industries played an important role in the ascent of the circus, and the demands of its diverse audiences bred innovation. The spectacular debut of Barnum's circus in 1871 and the combination of the nation's two largest shows into the Ringling Bros. and Barnum & Bailey Circus in 1919 serve as the bookends for Part III, *The Golden Age of the Circus in New York*. By the end of the nineteenth century, the circus was the most popular form of entertainment in the United States, a restless and industrial enterprise that was a cultural metonym of modernity. During these years, the brightly colored circus posters that

heralded the arrival of the Barnum & Bailey Circus were the city's first sign of spring, and the opening performance at Madison Square Garden was a national event. At its height, more than a million people attended annually to enjoy the overwhelming sights and sounds, the spectacle of the American circus. Part IV, *Scenes from the Twentieth Century*, looks at the relative decline of the circus in New York City, as competition and fragmentation ate away at its predominant position in the world of entertainment. Still, the Ringling Bros. and Barnum & Bailey Circus continues its annual visit, and the vibrant "new circus" movement has ensured that the circus remains part of the city's cultural milieu.[7]

The catalogue of the exhibition features entries for a select group of objects ranging from circus posters to props and wardrobe. These intriguing things reveal the showmanship, skill, and creativity of the circus, highlighting the performers and entrepreneurs who have made the circus a thriving American spectacle for more than two centuries. The contemporary texts reprinted in the appendix offer unique insights into how New York writers and critics experienced the circus.

The exhibition and catalogue document the rise, apogee, and fragmentation of the American circus in New York City over the last two hundred years, highlighting the ways in which the two phenomena shaped each other and calling attention to the rich cultural heritage and varied legacy of the circus.

1 The first comprehensive effort to write the history of the circus in the United States was undertaken by T. Alston Brown and serialized in the *New York Clipper* between December 20, 1860, and February 9, 1861, as "A Complete History of the Amphitheatre and Circus from Its Earliest Date to 1861." This series was usefully edited and republished by William L. Slout as *Amphitheatres and Circuses: A History from Their Earliest Date to 1861, with Sketches of Some of the Principal Performers* (San Bernardino, CA: Borgo Press, 1994). Noteworthy general histories of the American circus include, Isaac J. Greenwood, *The Circus: Its Origin and Growth Prior to 1835* (New York: The Dunlap Society, 1898); Earl Chapin May, *The Circus from Rome to Ringling* (New York: Duffield and Green, 1932); John Durant and Alice K. R. Durant, *Pictorial History of the American Circus* (New York: A. S. Barnes, 1957); George L. Chindahl, *A History of the Circus in America* (Caldwell, ID: Caxton Printers, 1959); George Speaight, *A History of the Circus* (London: Tantivy Press, 1980). For more recent work by circus enthusiasts and historians, see John Culhane, *The American Circus: An Illustrated History* (New York: Holt, 1990); David Carlyon, *Dan Rice: The Most Famous Man You've Never Heard Of* (New York: Public Affairs, 2001); Stuart Thayer, *Annals of the American Circus, 1793–1860* (Seattle: Dauven and Thayer, 2001); Janet M. Davis, *The Circus Age: Culture and Society under the American Big Top* (Chapel Hill: University of North Carolina Press, 2002); S. L. Kotar and J. E. Gessler, *The Rise of the American Circus, 1716–1899* (Jefferson, NC: McFarland & Company, 2011). For a collection of critical essays exploring the concept of Americanization, see the companion volume to this catalogue: Susan Weber, Kenneth L. Ames, and Matthew Wittmann, eds., *The American Circus* (New York and New Haven: Yale University Press for the Bard Graduate Center, 2012).

2 "The Elephants Cross the Bridge," *New York Times*, May 18, 1884.

3 The exception to this rule was George C. Odell, who rather begrudgingly documented the history of the circus as part of his comprehensive fifteen-volume study of popular entertainment in New York City: *Annals of the New York Stage,* 16 vols. (New York: Columbia University Press, 1927–49).

4 The Museum of the City of New York and the New-York Historical Society have each mounted two major circus exhibitions: *The Circus: From Noah's Ark to New York* (MCNY, 1938); *Circus Time* (NYHS, 1953); *P. T. Barnum: Prince of Humbug, Merchant of Delight* (NYHS, 1986); *Under the Big Top: Circuses in New York* (MCNY, 1997–98).

5 For a recent and useful introduction to various conceptual approaches to popular culture, see James W. Cook and Lawrence B. Glickman, "Twelve Propositions for a History of U.S. Cultural History," *The Cultural Turn in U.S. History: Past, Present, and Future* (Chicago: University of Chicago Press, 2008), 3–58. For a classic and still informative exchange on the subject, see Lawrence Levine, "The Folklore of Industrial Society: Popular Culture and Its Audiences," *American Historical Review* 97, no. 5 (December 1992), 1369–99; and three responses to Levine: Robin D. G. Kelley, "Notes on Deconstructing the Folk," 1400–1408; Natalie Zemon Davis, "Toward Mixtures and Margins," 1409–16; Jackson Lears, "Making Fun of Popular Culture," 1417–26. For an astute survey, see Michael G. Kammen, *American Culture, American Tastes: Social Change and the 20th Century* (New York: Knopf, 1999).

6 Davis, *The Circus Age*, xiii; Paul Bouissac, *Circus and Culture: A Semiotic Approach* (Bloomington: Indiana University Press, 1976).

7 Because of renovations at Madison Square Garden, the Ringling Bros. and Barnum & Bailey Circus did not perform in New York City in 2011–12, although it will resume playing its annual spring dates there in 2013.

Chronology of New York City and the Circus
Compiled by Alexis Mucha

1623–24

The first permanent European settlements are established in the New York region, where the indigenous Lenape people are living.

1664

August 27: Nieuw Amsterdam becomes New York when English soldiers take the town on orders from Charles II.

1732

December 6: A troupe of actors from London presents the earliest documented performance of a play, entitled *The Recruiting Officer*, at a repurposed warehouse on Maiden Lane and Pearl Street.

1768

Philip Astley originates the modern circus in London with multi-act exhibitions in a circular ring that feature acrobats, rope-dancers, clowns, and equestrian performers.

1771–72

A "Mr. Faulks" gives equestrian exhibitions on an enclosed piece of ground behind the Wind-Mill on Bowery Lane.

1774

The Continental Congress abolishes theatrical activities and recommends closing all places of amusement. The John Street Theatre promptly shuts down.

1776

August 27: British forces defeat the Continental Army in the Battle of Long Island,

and the city falls two days later.

1783

November 25: The last British troops withdraw from the city, and George Washington and his troops march down Broadway; November 25 will become the holiday known as Evacuation Day.

1785

The city's first daily newspaper, the *New-York Daily Advertiser*, begins publication.

1786

An American named Pool builds a structure on Rutgers Hill near Maiden Lane, with seating for equestrian displays, and advertises a clown to entertain between feats.

1790

August 12: Congress meets in Manhattan for the last time before relocating to the new capital in Philadelphia.

1793

August 7: John Bill Ricketts establishes the first circus in New York City on Greenwich Street.

Fig. C.1

1795

March: Native American riders billed as "Indian Chiefs" perform in Ricketts's Circus.

1796

April 14: The first elephant is imported to the United States from Bengal by Captain Jacob Crowninshield and is displayed on Beaver Street and Broadway.

1797

March: John Bill Ricketts holds his circus season in a new ampitheater on Greenwich Street designed by Joseph-François Mangin.

1798

January: The New Theatre, later the Park Theatre, on Park Row opens, with seating for 1,200 patrons.

Fig. C.2

1804

The New-York Historical Society is founded to preserve and collect artifacts related to United States and New York State history.

1807

The first commercial steamboat begins regular service between Albany and New York City.

Washington Irving co-founds the satirical literary magazine *Salmagundi* and uses the moniker "Gotham" to describe the city.

1808

May 31: Victor Pepin and Jean Breschard host a circus in an open-air arena on Broadway and Magazine Street.

1810

P. T. Barnum is born in Bethel, Connecticut.

New York becomes the largest city in the United States.

1811

New York adopts a Commissioner's Plan to mark off future Manhattan streets and avenues in a grid formation.

1812

June 18: The United States declares war on Great Britain.

June 25: Cayetano Mariotini debuts a performing elephant in the ring at the New York Circus.

1814

December 24: The Treaty of Ghent is signed, ending the War of 1812.

Fig. C.3

1817

January 22: James West, a celebrated equestrian with the Royal Circus in London, arrives in New York to perform *Timour the Tartar*, an equestrian drama, at the Park Theatre.

February 25: The New York Stock and Exchange Board is established.

August: James West opens a "New Circus" on Broadway near Canal Street.

1822

August 10: Stephen Price and Edmund Simpson, owners of the Park Theatre, in an effort to vanquish their competition, instigate a riot at the African-American–owned African Theatre.

1825

J. Purdy Brown and Lewis Bailey begin to tour using a canvas tent, or "pavilion," for performances, moving the circus beyond wooden arenas in predominantly urban markets.

October 26: The Erie Canal opens, connecting the Great Lakes with the Atlantic Ocean via the Hudson River.

Fig. C.4

1826

October 23: The Bowery Theatre opens as the largest theater in the United States.

1827

July 4: Slavery is abolished in New York.

1829

April: New York City enacts a law requiring circus and theater managers and proprietors to obtain a license to operate.

September 13: The famed "Siamese Twins," Chang and Eng, debut at the Masonic Hall.

1832

November 12: Thomas Dartmouth Rice introduces the character Jim Crow as part of a blackface song-and-dance routine at the Bowery Theatre.

Fig. C.5

November 14: The New York and Harlem Railroad begins running horse cars that seat 40 along tracks from Prince Street to Fourth Avenue as far north as Harlem.

1834

December: The Zoological Institute of the City of New York opens at 37 Bowery, featuring the animal trainer Isaac Van Amburgh.

1835

December 16–17: The Great Fire destroys most of the buildings around Wall Street.

1837

The Zoological Institute at 37 Bowery closes and gives way to the Bowery Amphitheatre, which will serve as the primary venue for circus performances in the decade that follows.

September 23: Inventor Samuel F. B. Morse is granted a patent for his magnetic telegraph.

1840

Levi North completes the first back somersault on horseback in the United States at the Bowery Theatre.

John W. Draper produces the first successful portrait daguerreotype in New York after improving on Louis Daguerre's original plate.

1842

January 1: Barnum's American Museum opens on Broadway and Ann Street.

December 7: The New York Philharmonic presents its first concert.

1843

During February, the Virginia Minstrels perform at the Bowery Amphitheatre, establishing the minstrel show as one of the most popular forms of entertainment in New York.

New York's first public school is opened by the Board of Education.

1849

May 10: The Astor Place Riot, sparked by a dispute between the American actor Edwin Forrest and the English actor William Macready, leaves 22 dead and hundreds injured after the National Guard fires on an angry crowd gathered in the Astor Place Theatre.

Fig. C.6

1850

September 1: Singer Johanna Maria "Jenny" Lind, known as the "Swedish Nightingale," signs a contract with P. T. Barnum to tour the United States and creates a sensation upon her arrival in New York.

1853

The New York Clipper, a weekly newspaper devoted entirely to sports and entertainment, is founded.

May 2: Franconi's Hippodrome opens on Broadway and Twenty-Third Street near Madison Square as the largest show in the United States to date.

The Exhibition of the Industry of All Nations, the first U.S. world's fair, is held in the New York Crystal Palace, west of Fifth Avenue between Fortieth and Forty-second Streets.

Fig. C.7

1855

Walt Whitman publishes Leaves of Grass.

Castle Garden is transformed from a theater into an immigration center and occasional circus venue.

1858

October 27: R. H. Macy Company department store opens on Sixth Avenue south of Fourteenth Street.

Central Park opens to the public, although it is not yet complete.

Sands, Nathans & Co.'s American Circus parades through the city with a steam calliope.

1861

April 12: Forces of the Confederate States of America bombard Fort Sumter and the Civil War begins.

1863

February 10: P. T. Barnum's star General Tom Thumb marries fellow dwarf Lavinia Warren at Grace Church.

Fig. C.8

July 12: Draft riots break out in New York City and continue until July 17, leaving hundreds dead and wounded and causing millions in property damage.

1865

April 9: The Confederate Army led by General Robert E. Lee surrenders to General Ulysses S. Grant at Appomattox Court House in Virginia, ending the Civil War.

Lewis B. Lent takes over the New York Circus in the Hippotheatron on Fourteenth Street and Fourth Avenue. The building, which had opened the previous year, becomes the premier circus in New York.

July 13: P. T. Barnum's American Museum burns down.

1866

The American Society for the Prevention of Cruelty to Animals is founded in New York City.

1869

The American Museum of Natural History opens on Fifth Avenue and Sixty-fourth Street.

1871

Grand Central Depot opens on Vanderbilt Avenue and Forty-second Street.

April 10: P. T. Barnum's Great Traveling Museum, Menagerie, Caravan, and Hippodrome debuts under canvas in Brooklyn.

1872

The Metropolitan Museum of Art opens at 681 Fifth Avenue.

P. T. Barnum begins billing his show as "The Greatest Show on Earth" and exclusively touring by railroad.

1874

April 26: P. T. Barnum's Great Roman Hippodrome opens in the square between Madison and Fourth Avenues and Twenty-sixth and Twenty-seventh Streets.

1876

December 5: A fire breaks out backstage at the Brooklyn Theater, killing 295 people.

The National Baseball League is organized.

Fig. C.9

1881

P. T. Barnum and James A. Bailey unite their shows for the first time.

October 24: The "birth" of vaudeville occurs at Tony Pastor's Opera House on Union Square.

1882

April 9: The elephant Jumbo arrives in New York from London. "Jumbomania" ensues.

1883

May 24: The Brooklyn Bridge opens to traffic.

1885

Jumbo is killed by a freight train in St. Thomas, Ontario.

1886

October 28: The Statue of Liberty is dedicated by President Grover Cleveland, and the first ticker-tape parade is held the following day.

Fig. C.10

Buffalo Bill's Wild West Show opens in Madison Square Garden in November for a winter season.

1887

Adam Forepaugh and the Barnum & Bailey Circus present a combined show at Madison Square Garden.

1890

Madison Square Garden is purchased by J. P. Morgan and demolished to make way for a new Madison Square Garden designed by Stanford White of McKim, Mead, and White.

Jacob Riis publishes *How the Other Half Lives: Studies among the Tenements of New York.*

1891

April 7: P. T. Barnum dies at the age of 80.

Carnegie Hall opens on Seventh Avenue and Fifty-seventh Street.

1892

Madison Square Garden reopens as the largest indoor space of its kind in the United States.

Fig. C.11

January 1: Ellis Island opens to process immigrants, replacing Castle Clinton.

1894

Billboard magazine begins as an eight-page monthly.

1895

May 23: The New York Public Library is created by consolidating the Astor, Lenox, and Tilden Libraries.

1896

April 20: Koster and Bial's Music Hall hosts the first U.S. screening of motion pictures, as part of a vaudeville show.

1898

The City of New York is formally consolidated after a vote by the state legislature on May 4, 1897.

1899

November 8: The New York Zoological Society opens the Bronx Zoo.

1903

Barnum & Bailey return from Europe after a four-year tour abroad. The circus parade is discontinued in Manhattan.

May 16: Luna Park opens on Coney Island.

Fig. C.12

1904

October 27: The first major subway line opens, running from the Brooklyn Bridge to Forty-second Street, west to Broadway and north to 145th Street.

1905

April 12: The Hippodrome Theatre opens on Sixth Avenue between Forty-third and Forty-fourth Streets.

1906

April 11: James A. Bailey dies while the Barnum & Bailey Cirucs is performing its annual opening dates at Madison Square Garden.

1907

The Ringling Brothers acquire ownership of the Barnum & Bailey Circus.

May: Taximeter cabs appear in New York, replacing horse-drawn hansom cabs.

1909

The first large electric sign appears in Times Square.

Ringling Bros. Circus visits New York City for the first time.

1911

March 25: A fire in the Triangle Shirtwaist Company building kills 146 workers.

1912

May Wirth joins the Barnum & Bailey Circus as the world's greatest female bareback rider.

1913

The Armory Show introduces Cubism to the American public.

April 9: To prevent the Brooklyn Dodgers from moving to Baltimore, Ebbets Field opens in Brooklyn in a lot on Bedford and Belmont Avenues. The Dodgers will move to Los Angeles 45 years later, in 1958.

1914

July 28: The Austro-Hungarian Empire invades Serbia following the assassination of the Austrian Archduke Franz Ferdinand in June. The other major European powers join the conflict, invoking alliances formed in the previous decade.

The Strand Movie Theater opens as the largest movie theater in the country, with seating for 3,300.

1917

November 6: New York State adopts a constitutional amendment granting women the right to vote.

For the first time, there are more motor vehicles than horses on the streets of New York City.

1919

March 29: The combined Ringling Bros. and Barnum & Bailey Circus debuts at Madison Square Garden.

June 28: The Treaty of Versailles is signed, ending World War I.

1920

January 17: Prohibition goes into effect.

1922

March 2: The first radio station in New York City, WEAF, begins broadcasting.

1923

April 18: Yankee Stadium opens in the Bronx.

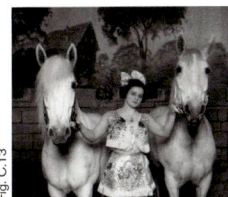
Fig. C.13

1924

November 27: Macy's holds its first big Christmas Day parade, which becomes the Macy's Thanksgiving Day Parade in 1935.

1925

Madison Square Garden is demolished, as a new Garden opens November 28 on Eighth Avenue between Forty-ninth and Fiftieth Streets.

1927

November 12: The Holland Tunnel opens, connecting lower Manhattan and Jersey City and providing an alternative to ferry service.

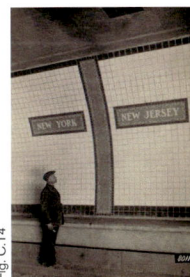
Fig. C.14

1928

April: The Wallendas make their American debut at Madison Square Garden.

1929

The stock market crashes, signaling the beginning of the Great Depression.

April: *The Circus in Paint* exhibition opens at the Whitney Studio Galleries.

November 8: The Museum of Modern Art opens on the eighth floor of the Heckscher Building at 730 Fifth Avenue.

1931

May 1: The Empire State Building, designed by William F. Lamb of Shreve, Lamb, and Harmon, opens as the world's tallest skyscraper.

1932

Homeless New Yorkers build a "Hoover Village" on the Hudson River at Seventy-fourth Street, in Central Park, and on the East River at Ninth Street.

John Ringling defaults on loans, and Samuel Gompertz takes over management of the Ringling's circuses.

October: Tiny Kline slides over 1,000 feet on a wire suspended above Times Square hanging by only a bit in her mouth.

1934

The School of American Ballet is founded with George Balanchine as the choreographer.

1935

The musical comedy *Jumbo*, with music and lyrics by Rogers and Hart, opens at the Hippodrome starring Jimmy Durante and a live elephant.

1935–39

The Works Progress Administration sponsors the Federal Theatre Project, which organizes a circus that puts to work unemployed performers and support personnel around the five boroughs.

1937

John Ringling North reasserts control over the various Ringling circuses.

1938

A labor dispute with the American Federation of Actors forces the Ringling Bros. and Barnum & Bailey Circus to end its season early.

1939

April 30: The New York World's Fair opens in Flushing Meadow Park, Queens. The opening ceremonies are televised by NBC onto experimental receivers that have been set up in the metropolitan area.

Fig. C.15

December 2: LaGuardia Airport opens on the east shore of Flushing Bay.

1941
Norman Bel Geddes is hired to redesign all aspects of the Ringling Bros. and Barnum & Bailey Circus.

December 7: Japanese airplanes attack the U.S. naval base at Pearl Harbor in the Hawaiian Islands, drawing the United States into World War II. Germany declares war on the United States December 11.

1942
George Balanchine and Igor Stravinsky collaborate on the "Ballet of the Elephants."

Fig. C.16

1945
August 14: The Japanese surrender is announced, ending World War II, and thousands gather to celebrate in Times Square.

Weegee's first book of photographs, *Naked City*, is published.

1947
Jackie Robinson signs with the Brooklyn Dodgers as the first black baseball player in the Major Leagues.

1950
The United Nations completes the Secretariat building with offices for 3,400 employees on an 18-acre campus in midtown Manhattan.

Fig. C.17

1951
RCA and CBS begin to broadcast television programs in color.

1952
Cecil B. DeMille's movie *The Greatest Show on Earth* is released.

1955
March 30: Marilyn Monroe opens the Ringling Bros. and Barnum & Bailey Circus at Madison Square Garden by riding in on a pink elephant.

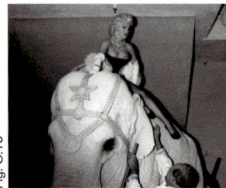
Fig. C.18

October: *The Village Voice* begins publication.

1956
July 16: The Ringling Bros. and Barnum & Bailey Circus strike the tents for the last time in Pittsburgh and moves to a strictly indoor operation.

1959
October 21: The Solomon R. Guggenheim Museum opens its new Frank Lloyd Wright building at 1071 Fifth Avenue.

1961
Jane Jacobs publishes *The Death and Life of Great American Cities* and rallies residents to block the proposed cross-Manhattan expressway.

July: Pennsylvania Railroad announces plans to replace Penn Station by building a new Madison Square Garden and office tower on top of a new railroad station.

1964
April 22: The New York World's Fair opens in Flushing Meadow Park, on the same site as the 1939 fair.

1966
August 5: Ground is broken for excavation of the World Trade Center; the landfill created will be used to create Battery Park City.

The theaters at Lincoln Center are completed.

Fig. C.19

1967
November: John Ringling North sells the Ringling Bros. and Barnum & Bailey Circus to music promoter Irvin Feld and partners.

1968
February 11: The new Madison Square Garden opens.

The Ringling Bros. and Barnum & Bailey Circus hires its first African-American feature act, the King Charles Troupe.

1969
June 27: The police raid the Stonewall Inn in Greenwich Village, which helps to launch the gay rights movement.

November: *Sesame Street* debuts on PBS.

1971
The Ringling Bros. and Barnum & Bailey elephants walk into the city through the Lincoln Tunnel because of a rail strike.

New York City becomes known as "The Big Apple" as part of a publicity campaign organized by the New York Convention and Visitors Bureau, reviving a nickname popularized 40 years earlier.

1973
April 4: The World Trade Center is formally dedicated.

1974
August 7: Philippe Petit, a French daredevil, secretly stretches a cable between the World Trade Center towers and walks across it.

1977
July 13: A 25-hour power failure hits the city after

lightning strikes north of the city, knocking out lines that feed into Consolidated Edison's power grid. Looting takes place in impoverished neighborhoods.

July 19: The Big Apple Circus debuts its one-ring circus in Battery Park City.

The Wells, Rich, Greene advertising agency creates the "I love New York" slogan to promote the city.

1980
April 20: The Broadway musical *Barnum* opens, with music by Cy Coleman and lyrics by Michael Stewart.

1981
December: The Big Apple Circus moves to its current home in Damrosch Park at Lincoln Center.

1983
April 30: Ringling Bros. and Barnum & Bailey Circus hosts the "Circus for Life, The Biggest Gay Event of All Time," a benefit at Madison Square Garden to support the Gay Men's Health Crisis in the fight against AIDS; $300,000 is raised during a sold-out performance.

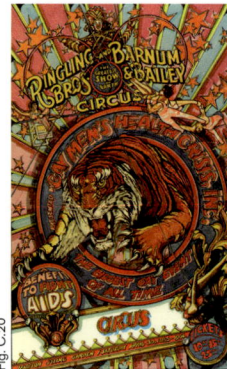
Fig. C.20

1985
The Big Apple Circus begins to tour beyond New York City.

1988
Cirque du Soleil debuts in a tent erected in Battery Park.

Fig. C.21

1997
The African-American–oriented UniverSoul Circus first performs in Harlem.

2001
September 11: Two commercial airliners are hijacked by terrorists and flown into the World Trade Center, causing the two towers to collapse.

2011
Because of renovations at Madison Square Garden, the Ringling Bros. and Barnum & Bailey Circus does not perform in New York City for the first time in over a century.

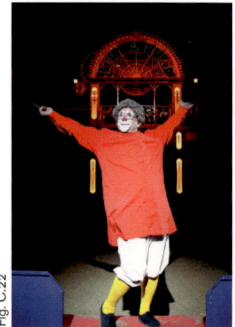
Fig. C.22

Barry Lubin has his last season as Grandma the Clown with the Big Apple Circus.

"It is a season of still deeper excitement, in such a retired country village, when once a year, after several days' heralding, a train of great red wagons is seen approaching, marked in large letters, CIRCUS..."
—*The Knickerbocker*, 1839

Checklist of the Exhibition

6

7   9

15

1. THE EARLY YEARS

1 *John Bill Ricketts*
Gilbert Stuart (1755–1828)
1795–99
Oil on canvas
29 3/8 × 24 1/4 in.
(74.6 × 61.5 cm)
National Gallery of Art, Gift of Mrs. Robert Noyes in memory of Elisha Riggs, 1942.14.1
See cat. entry 1.

2 "Ricketts's Circus" token
ca. 1795
Silver
U.S. Mint, Philadelphia
28.7 mm
The American Numismatic Society, ANS 1903.27.1
See fig. 1.2.

3 "New-York Circus, Corner of Broadway and White-st. … June 27, 1812."
1812
Broadside
Pelsue and Gould, Printers, New York
14 1/8 × 8 7/8 in.
(35.9 × 22.6 cm)
The New-York Historical Society
See fig. 1.6.

4 *Broadway Circus and Olympic Theatre, Broadway between Howard and Grand Streets, New York*
Anonymous American
after 1866
Watercolor and ink
14 3/8 × 12 in.
(36.5 × 30.5 cm)
The Metropolitan Museum of Art, New York, Museum Accession, transferred

from the Library, 1921
(21.36.236)
See fig. 1.7.

5 "The Elephant"
1797
Broadside with woodcut illustration
Printed by William Barrett, Newburyport, Massachusetts
9 1/2 × 7 5/8 in. closed
(24.2 × 19.4 cm)
The New-York Historical Society
See fig. 1.5.

6 Tusk chain
early 19th century
Iron
L. 56 n; th. 3 in.; cuff: 5 in.
(142.3 cm; 7.7 cm; 12.7 cm)
Somers Historical Society

7 Bull hook
early 19th century
Iron, wood
23 in. (58.5 cm)
Somers Historical Society

8 Trunk lined with a circus broadside
Chester Ellsworth
1828
Wood, metal, leather, horsehide, and paper
9 × 18 × 10 1/2 in.
(22.9 × 45.8 × 26.7 cm)
New York State Museum, Albany, H-1980.3.1
See cat. entry 2.

9 Rhinoceros horn
ca. 1830
Horn
26 in. (66.1 cm)
Somers Historical Society

10 Drum
Attributed to June, Titus, Avengine & Co.
ca. 1835
Painted wood, rope
24 × 52 in. (61 × 132.1 cm)
Somers Historical Society,

Gift of Laura Howe Nelson, 75.0.5
See fig. 2.2.

11 "Magnanimity of the Elephant Displayed in the Preservation of his Keeper J. Martin, in the Bowery Menagerie in New York"
1835
Etching and aquatint
15 × 21 in.
(38.1 × 53.4 cm)
Somers Historical Society, 91.19.1
See fig. 1.8.

12 "The Association's Celebrated and Extensive Menagerie and Aviary from their Zoological Institute in the City of New-York"
1835
Poster with woodcut illustrations
Printed by Jared W. Bell, New York
109 × 77 in.
(276.9 × 195.6 cm)
Shelburne Museum, Shelburne, Vermont, Gift of Harry T. Peters Sr. Family, 1959, 1959-67
See cat. entry 4.

13 *Portrait of Mr Van Amburgh, As He Appeared with His Animals at the London Theatres*
Sir Edwin Henry Landseer (1802–1873)
1846–47
Oil on canvas
69 1/4 × 94 in.
(175.9 × 238.8 cm)
Yale Center for British Art, Paul Mellon Collection, B1977.14.61
See cat. entry 5.

14 "Descriptive Sheet of Banigan and Kelley's Popular Menagerie for 1847: Newly Fitted and Direct from

La Fayette Place, City of New York."
1847
Poster with woodcut illustrations, printed in three colors
Engraved by T. W. Strong, New York; printed by Jared W. Bell, New York
47 × 96 in.
(119.4 × 243.9 cm)
New York State Museum, Albany
See fig. 2.4.

15 "The Only Living Giraffe in America"
1863
Color lithograph
Sarony, Major & Knapp, New York
17½ × 12 in.
(44.5 × 30.5 cm)
Shelburne Museum, Shelburne, Vermont, Gift of Harry T. Peters Sr. Family, 1959, 1959-67.81

16 Barnum's American Museum
ca. 1850–53
Lithograph
Lithograph by Brown and Severin, New York; printed by G. W. Lewis III, New York
23½ × 30 in.
(59.7 × 76.2 cm)
Collection of the Barnum Museum
See fig. 2.7.

17 "Barnum's American Museum. Entertainments in the Lecture Room Every Afternoon and Evening. Saturday, July 14, 1855."
1855
Two-sided herald with woodcut illustration
Daily Times Job Office–M. B. Wynkoop, Book and Job Printer, New York
24 × 9 in. (61 × 22.9 cm)
The John and Mable Ringling Museum of Art, Tibbals Collection, ht4000046a

18 P. T. Barnum's American Museum medal
ca. 1855–60
White metal
Allen and Moore, Philadelphia
40 mm
The New-York Historical Society, Gift of Bella C. Landauer, 2002.1.4430

19 P. T. Barnum top hat
ca. 1830s
Felted fur (rabbit)

Label: "Ezra S. Hamilton, Hat, Cap, and Fur Store, 200 Main Street, Hartford, Conn."
8 × 13 × 14 in.
(20.4 × 33.1 × 35.6 cm)
Collection of the Barnum Museum, 1971.2.1

20 *P. T. Barnum*
ca. 1885
Albumen print
London Stereoscopic & Photographic Company
13 × 7⅜ in.
(33.1 × 18.8 cm)
Collection of the Barnum Museum, 2007.9.55

21 "Barnum's Collection of Curiosities."
ca. 1864–69
Poster with woodcut illustrations
Engraved by Waters & Son, New York; printed by Thos. McIlroy & Co., New York
25⅛ × 20¾ in.
(63.9 × 52.8 cm)
Shelburne Museum, Shelburne, Vermont, Gift of Harry T. Peters Sr. Family, 1959, 1959-67.114
See fig. 2.11.

22 "Vantile Mack, the Infant Lambert, or Giant Baby!!"
ca. 1860
Hand-colored lithograph
Currier & Ives, New York
12 × 9 in. (30.5 × 22.9 cm)
Shelburne Museum, Shelburne, Vermont, 1959-67.6
See fig. 2.12.

23 "Barnum's Gallery of Wonders. No. 14. The Wonderful Albino Family."
ca. 1860
Hand-colored lithograph
Currier & Ives, New York
14 × 10 in.
(35.6 × 25.4 cm)
Shelburne Museum, Shelburne, Vermont, 1959-7.4

24 "'Chang' and 'Eng,' The World Renowned United Siamese Twins."
1860
Hand-colored lithograph
Currier & Ives, New York
16 × 11½ in.
(40.7 × 29.3 cm)
Shelburne Museum, Shelburne, Vermont, Gift of Harry T. Peters Sr. Family, 1959, 1959-67.11

25 P. T. Barnum and General Tom Thumb
Samuel Root (1819–1889) and Marcus Aurelius Root (1808–1888)
ca. 1850
Half-plate daguerreotype
Case open: 6¼ × 9¾ × ½ in. (15.4 × 24.8 × 1.3 cm); plate: 5½ × 4¼ in. (14 × 10.8 cm)
National Portrait Gallery, Smithsonian Institution, NPG.93.154
See fig. 2.8.

26 "American Museum / Every Day & Evening This Week / Commencing Monday, March 1st, 1847 . . . General Tom Thumb!"
1847
Herald with woodcut illustration
Applegate's Steam Presses, New York
24 × 9 in. (61 × 22.9 cm)
The New-York Historical Society, PR-055

27 "Gen. Tom Thumb In His different Characters."
ca. 1860
Photographs adhered to a printed board
Photographs with hand-drawn additions by E. T. Whitney and Co., Norwalk, Conn.
13¾ × 9½ in.
(35 × 24.2 cm)
Collection of the Barnum Museum, EL 1988.84.1
See fig. 2.9.

28 General Tom Thumb (Charles S. Stratton) suit
1840s
Silk velvet, modern silk lining
21 × 19½ in.
(53.4 × 49.6 cm)
Collection of the Barnum Museum, T2008.5.AB
See fig. 2.10.

29 General Tom Thumb (Charles S. Stratton) pair of boots
1840s–50s
Leather
6⅝ × 5¼ in.
(16.9 × 13.4 cm)
Collection of the Barnum Museum, EL 1988.117.1AB

30 General Tom Thumb (Charles S. Stratton) violin and bow
1845
Wood (pine or spruce),

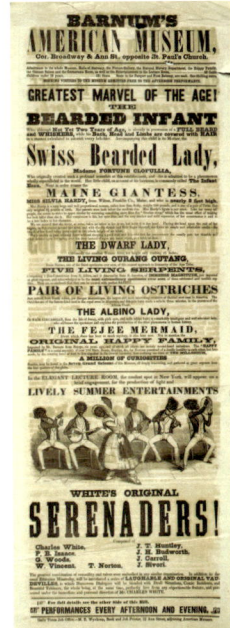
17

18

19

20

23

24

26

30

34

39

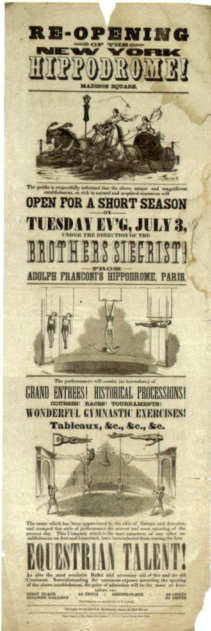

40

43

42

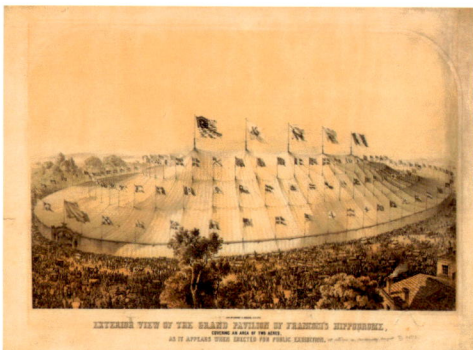

44

various materials
Violin: 15¾ × 5¼ × 1¼ in.;
bow: 18¼ × ¼ in. (violin:
40.1 × 13.4 × 3.2 cm; bow:
46.4 × 0.7 cm)
Hertzberg Circus Collection
of the Witte Museum, San
Antonio, Texas, 2003-7 G

31 "Genl. Tom Thumb
& Wife, Com. Nutt &
Minnie Warren. Four
Wondrously Formed &
Strangely Beautiful Ladies
& Gentlemen in Miniatures,
Natures Smallest Editions of
Her Choicest Works.
The Greatest Wonders in
the World."
1863
Hand-colored lithograph
Currier & Ives, New York
13¾ × 17½ in.
(35 × 44.5 cm)
Shelburne Museum,
Shelburne, Vermont, Gift of
Harry T. Peters Sr. Family,
1959, 1959-67.20
See chronology, fig. C.8.

2. THE AMERICAN CIRCUS COMES OF AGE

32 "Mr. Sage, Proprietor of
the Great American Circus
from the City of New York"
1843
Poster with woodcut illustrations, printed in three colors
122 × 82 in.
(310 × 208 cm)
Shelburne Museum,
Shelburne, Vermont,
1960-134
See fig. 2.3.

33 Ringmaster vest
mid-19th century
Striped silk with milk-glass
buttons
L. 21 in.; w. 17 in.
(53.4; 43.2 cm)
Somers Historical Society,
95.18.1
See fig. 1.9.

34 Ringmaster pants
mid-19th century

Linen
L. 38 in.; waist: 32 in.
(96.6; 81.3 cm)
Somers Historical Society,
95.18.2

35 Ringmaster top hat
mid-19th century
Felted fur
Label: "Stephens"
6⅞ × 8⅞ in.
(17.5 × 22.5 cm)
Somers Historical Society,
95.18.3
See fig. 1.9.

36 Globe used by Jacob A.
Showles (1826–1912)
ca. 1860
Graduated wood with
painted cloth cover
Diam. 26 in. (66.1 cm)
Circus World Museum,
CWi-2652
See cat. entry 8.

37 "Circus / Bowery
Amphitheatre. Thanksgiving
Day. Three performances!"
1844
Herald with woodcut illustra-
tions
23½ × 18 in. (59.7 × 45.7 cm)
The John and Mabel Ringling
Museum of Art Archives,
RMA220.163
See fig. 2.6.

38 Box ticket for June, Titus,
Avengine & Co. Menagerie
and Circus at the Bowery
Amphitheatre
ca. 1840
Signed "Lewis B. Lent"
on verso
Ink on paper
1½ × 3⅛ in. (3.9 × 8 cm)
Somers Historical Society
See fig. 2.5.

39 Box pass for the Bowery
Amphitheatre
ca. 1842
Ink on paper
2½ × 3⅝ in. (6.4 × 9.3 cm)
Somers Historical Society

40 "Henri Franconi and His
Horse Bayard—Opening
Night, N.Y. Hippodrome."
from the *Illustrated News*,
May 14, 1853
Engraving
8 × 12 in. (20.4 × 30.5 cm)
Somers Historical Society,
73.24.20

41 "Franconi Schottisch /
Composed for the Piano
Forte and respectfully dedi-

cated to the Visitors of the
Hippodrome"
Franklin L. Harris, composer
1853
Tinted lithograph
Lithograph by Sarony &
Major, New York; published
by T.S. Berry, New York
10½ × 13¼ in.
(26.7 × 33.7 cm)
Somers Historical Society,
94.1.9
See fig. 2.13.

42 "Exterior View of
Franconi's Colossal
Hippodrome / Sketch of
the Interior of Franconi's
Hippodrome"
1853
Lithograph courier
Strong Lith., New York
13 × 18 in.
(33.1 × 45.8 cm)
Somers Historical Society,
95.19.87

43 "Exterior View of the
Grand Pavilion of Franconi's
Hippodrome, Covering an
Area of Two Acres, as it
Appears When Erected for
Public Exhibition."
1853
Inscription: "at Utica on
Wednesday August 17th,
1853"
Tinted lithograph
Sarony & Major, New York
30¼ × 43 in. (77 × 109 cm)
Courtesy American
Antiquarian Society

44 "Re-opening of the New
York Hippodrome! Madison
Square….Open for a Short
Season on Tuesday Ev'g,
July 3, under the Direction
of the Brothers Seigrist!"
1855
Herald with woodcut
illustrations
Engraved by E. Purcell;
printed by Frank Farwell &
Co., Steam Job Printers,
New York
29⅞ × 10⅜ in.
(75.9 × 26.4 cm)
The John and Mable Ringling
Museum of Art, Tibbals
Collection, ht4000675

45 *Dan Rice*
Leonard Welles Volk
(1828–1895)
1863
Marble
9¼ × 24 × 27 in.
(23.5 × 61 × 68.6 cm)
Hertzberg Circus Collection

of the Witte Museum, San Antonio, Texas, 2003-7 G
See cat. entry 10.

46 Rosewood sword cane
J. E. Glover, New Orleans
1848
Inscribed on top of handle: "DR"; inscribed on sides of handle: "Presented to Dan Rice / By R. E. Hammet / of New Orleans / Dec. 20th 1848."
Rosewood, steel, and gold
36½ × 1½ in.
(92.8 × 3.9 cm)
Albany Institute of History & Art, Gift of Phoebe Powell Bender, 2003.30

47 "The Wonderful Elephant Lalla Rookh as She Appears in Dan Rices' Great Show."
1859
Inscription: "Worcester June 21st 1859, Monday"
Poster with woodcut illustrations, printed in three colors
Jno. E. Bacon, Printer and Engraver, New York
55 × 81 in.
(139.8 × 205.8 cm)
Courtesy American Antiquarian Society
See cat. entry 9.

48 "Dan Rice. 'The King of American Clowns.'"
ca. 1860
Lithograph
11½ × 9 in. (29.3 × 22.9)
Shelburne Museum, Shelburne, Vermont, Rare-C 791.309 Greenwood
See fig. 2.18.

49 Dan Rice striped pants
ca. 1860
Silksatin with velvet trim
L. 40 in.; waist: 31 in.
(101.7; 78.8 cm)
Hertzberg Circus Collection of the Witte Museum, San Antonio, Texas, 2003-7 G
See fig. 2.19.

50 "The Wonderfull & Beautifully Trained Horse Excelsior as He Actually Appears in Dan Rice's Great Show."
1867
Inscription: "Presented to Jackson Shackelford / By his Friend, Dan Rice"
Color lithograph poster
Sarony, Major & Knapp, New York
40 × 28½ in.
(101.7 × 72.4 cm)

Shelburne Museum, Shelburne, Vermont, Gift of Harry T. Peters Sr. Family, 1959, 1959-67.155

51 "Niblo's Garden / Nixon & Co's Great Troupe . . . Re-Engagement of the Original Humorist, Dan Rice Who is on His Farewell Tour Through the United States."
1859
Herald with woodcut illustration
Herald Print, New York
22 × 9 in. (55.9 × 22.9 cm)
The John and Mable Ringling Museum of Art, Tibbals Collection, ht4000678

52 *Lewis B. Lent*
Anonymous
ca. 1870
Oil on canvas
39 × 32 in.
(99.1 × 81.3 cm)
Somers Historical Society, Gift of Arthur McElroy, 97.40

53 "The New York Circus, L. B. Lent, Director."
ca. 1870
Albumen print on board with hand-drawn additions and color
13¾ × 17¼ in.
(35 × 43.9 cm)
Circus World Museum, CWi-2344

54 "New York Circus" token
ca. 1870
Silvered brass
T. N. Hickcox & Co., New York
36 mm
The American Numismatic Society, ANS 0000.999.41980

55 "New York Circus / Robert Stickney / Pittsburg, Monday, Tuesday & Wednesday, Aug. 30th, 31st & Sept. 1st."
1869
Color lithograph poster
Hatch & Co., New York
22 × 18 in.
(55.9 × 45.8 cm)
Somers Historical Society, 73.16.476

56 "The New York Circus Brass and Reed Band in Their Gorgeous Uniform of the French Imperial Cent Garde. . . . At Lowell, Monday, May 16th, 1870."
Henry Louis Stephens

(1824–1882)
1870
Color lithograph poster
Duval Steam Lithographic Co., Philadelphia
23 × 35 in. (58.5 × 89 cm)
Collection of Fred D. Pfening III
See cat. entry 11.

57 Bandwagon arriving at the Hippotheatron, New York
1870
Color lithograph poster
21 × 33 in.
(53.4 × 83.9 cm)
Hertzberg Circus Collection of the Witte Museum, San Antonio, Texas, 2003-7 G
See cat. entry 11.

58 "L. B. Lent's New York Circus / Mdlle. Carlotta De Berg, The Celebrated Equestrienne."
1866
Engraving
16 × 19 in. (40.7 × 48.3 cm)
Somers Historical Society, 78.0.16.561

59 "L. B. Lent's New York Circus from its Palatial Iron Edifice, New York City . . . Will Exhibit at Elgin, Ill. Tuesday, May 23"
1876
Herald with woodcut illustrations, printed in three colors
Engraved by Morse
13⅝ × 4½ in.
(34.6 × 11.4 cm)
The John and Mable Ringling Museum of Art, Tibbals Collection, ht4000671

60 "Nixon & Cos. Mammoth Circus / The Great Australian Rider James Melville as He Appeared Before the Press of New York in His Opening Rehearsal at Niblo's Garden."
1859
Inscription: "Providence May 23rd & 24th"
Tinted lithograph
Sarony, Major & Knapp, New York
88 × 68 in.
(223.6 × 172.8 cm)
Courtesy American Antiquarian Society
See page 8.

61 "Welch, Mann & Delevan's National Circus Band Carriage, Passing Up Broadway New York June 7th, 1845."

46

50

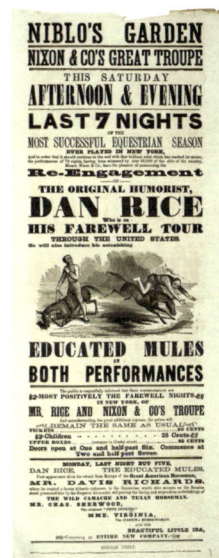
51

52

53

54

55

58

59

63

65

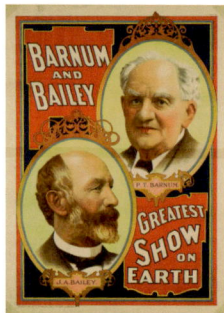

71

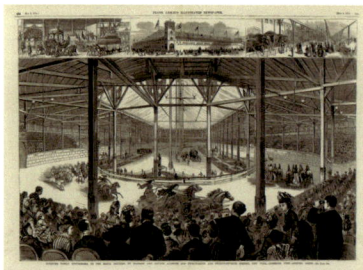

73

77

79

G. T. Sanford
1845
Inscription: "Massillon Wednesday Afternoon June 17th one Day Only"
Tinted lithograph
G. & W. Endicott, New York
26 × 39½ in.
(66.5 × 100.5 cm)
Courtesy American Antiquarian Society
See cat. entry 6.

62 "Grand Procession of the Steam Calliope Drawn by a Team of Six Elephants in the City of New York. Now Attached to Sand's, Nathan's & Co.s American & English Circus."
1858
Inscription: "Camden Monday Oct. 11th"
Color lithograph poster
Sarony, Major & Knapp, New York
30½ × 40½ in.
(77.5 × 102.9 cm)
The New-York Historical Society
See cat. entry 7.

63 "Van Amburgh & Co.s Tuba-Rheda."
Chas. Parsons
ca. 1865
Color lithograph poster
G. & W. Endicott, New York
30 × 45½ × 1 in.
(76.2 × 115.6 × 2.6 cm)
New York State Museum, Albany, H-1985.34.3

64 "Van Amburgh & Co.s Great Golden Car of Egypt. Living Lion Loose in the Street. Passing City Hall, New York"
1867
Inscription: "Monticello April 26th"
Color lithograph poster
Endicott & Co., New York
30 × 24 in. (76.2 × 61 cm)
Somers Historical Society, 73.16.227
See fig. 2.16.

65 "Van Amburgh & Co.s Great Golden Chariot. Passing Union Square, New York"
1867
Inscription: "Monticello April 26th"
Color lithograph poster
Endicott & Co, New York
30 × 24 in. (76.2 × 61 cm)
Somers Historical Society, 75.16.230

3.
THE GOLDEN AGE

66 Letter from P. T. Barnum to Moses Kimball, February 18, 1871
Engraved letterhead, ink on paper
8.5 × 5.125 in.
(21.6 × 13.2 cm)
Shelburne Museum, Shelburne, Vermont, MS 398 Peters Collection
See fig. 3.1.

67 "I Am Coming"
1875/1879
Framed poster with woodcut illustrations, printed in two colors
Inset portrait of P.T. Barnum engraved by Mayes; border by Roylance & Purcell, New York
Diam. 36 in. (91.5 cm)
Hertzberg Circus Collection of the Witte Museum, San Antonio, Texas
See fig. 3.6.

68 "P.T. Barnum's Museum and Menagerie" ticket
1871
Ink on paper
1¾ × 3¼ in. (4.5 × 8.3 cm)
Collection of the Barnum Museum, EL1988.22.1
See fig. 3.2.

69 *P. T. Barnum's Advance Courier*
1871
Illustrated newspaper
Engraved by Roylance & Purcell, New York; printed by Wynkoop & Hallenbeck, Steam Book and Job Printers, New York
14 × 10½ in.
(35.6 × 26.7 cm)
Somers Historical Society, 73.16.246
See fig. 3.3.

70 "Exterior View of Our Great City of Tents… Literal Scenes Taken from a Photograph, of the 3 Rings, Racing Track & Interior View of the 7 United Monster Shows."
1882
Color lithograph poster
Strobridge Lithographing Co., Cincinnati & New York
26 × 76 in.

(66.1 × 193.1 cm)
Somers Historical Society, Hugh Grant Rowell Collection, 73.16.225
See fig. 3.7.

71 "Barnum & Bailey Greatest Show on Earth / P. T. Barnum. / J. A. Bailey."
1897
Color lithograph poster
Strobridge Lithographing Co., Cincinnati & New York
39½ × 30 in.
(100.4 × 76.2 cm)
Collection of the Barnum Museum, 1990.37

72 Barnum's Roman Hippodrome
ca. 1874
Color lithograph poster
16 × 23¾ in.
(40.6 × 60.3 cm)
The John and Mable Ringling Museum of Art, Tibbals Collection, ht2004437
See fig. 3.4.

73 "Barnum's Roman Hippodrome, on the Block Bounded by Madison and Fourth Avenues and Twenty-sixth and Twenty-seventh Streets, New York.–Interior View–Opening Scene." From *Frank Leslie's Illustrated Newspaper*, May 9, 1874, pp. 136–37
1874
Print, wood engraving
16 × 22⅜ in.
(40.7 × 56.9 cm)
New York State Museum, Albany, H-1978.177.3

74 *Panorama of Barnum's Roman Hippodrome and Grand Procession of the Congress of Nations Zoological Institute Caravan and Museum*
1874
Pamphlet
Torrey Brothers, Printers, New York
6 × 4½ in.; folded out: 102 × 4½ in. (15.3 × 11.5; 259.1 × 11.5 cm)
Somers Historical Society, 94.1.33
See fig. 3.5.

75 *The Circus*
A. Logan
1874
Oil on canvas
24¼ × 38¼ in.
(61.6 × 97.2 cm)
Whitney Museum of

American Art, New York,
Gift of Edgar William and
Bernice Chrysler Garbisch,
D.69.147
See cat. entry 12.

76 *P. T. Barnum & Co's.
Greatest Show on Earth
and the Great, London
Circus United with Adam
Forepaugh's New and
Greatest All Feature Show.*
1887
Color lithograph courier
Courier Co., Buffalo
14 × 21 in.
(35.6 × 53.4 cm)
Collection of Fred D. Pfening III
See cat. entry 16.

77 "P. T. Barnum & Co's
Great Shows and Adam
Forepaugh's Colossal
Aggregation Combined…"
ticket
Ink on paper
2½ × 5 in. (6.4 × 12.7 cm)
Private collection

78 "Forepaugh & Sells
Brothers Enormous Shows
United / Madison Square
Garden New York. The
World Famous Metropolitan
Home of These Combined
Stupendous Shows."
1900
Color lithograph poster
Strobridge Lithographing
Co., Cincinnati & New York
29 × 39¾ in.
(73.7 × 101 cm)
Shelburne Museum,
Shelburne, Vermont, 1959-
259.13
See chronology, fig. C.11.

79 "Madison Square Garden
for a Brief Season Only
Beginning Thursday March
19th. The Barnum and Bailey
Greatest Show on Earth"
1908
Color lithograph poster
Strobridge Lithographing
Co., Cincinnati & New York
30 × 40 in.
(76.2 × 101.6 cm)
The John and Mabel Ringling
Museum of Art, Tibbals
Collection, ht2000285

80 "First Time in New York
/ Ringling Bros' World's
Greatest Shows"
1909
Color lithograph poster
Donaldson Lithographic Co.,
Newport, Ken.
39¾ × 26¼ in.

(101 × 66.7 cm)
The John and Mable Ringling
Museum of Art, Tibbals
Collection, ht2001294
See fig. 3.20.

81 Set of twelve photo-
graphic plates of Ringling
Bros. Circus parade in
Brooklyn
1909
Dry plate negatives
Obrig Camera Co., New
York
3¼ × 4¼ in.
(8.3 × 10.8 cm)
Somers Historical Society,
91.17.2
See cat. entry 20.

82 "Ringling Bros. World's
Greatest Shows" pennant
1911
Felt on bamboo cane
5½ × 14 in. (14 × 35.6 cm);
cane: 28½ in. (72.4 cm)
Circus World Museum,
CWi-2638

83 Jumbo handkerchief
ca.1882
Printed cotton
23⅝ × 21 in.
(60.1 × 53.4 cm)
Collection of the Barnum
Museum, 2005.3.1

84 "Jumbo / The Children's
Giant Pet."
1882
Color lithograph poster
Hatch Lithographic
Company, New York
48 × 30½ in.
(121.9 × 77.5 cm)
The John and Mable Ringling
Museum of Art, Tibbals
Collection, ht2004500
See cat. entry 14.

85 Lidded bowl in "Jumbo"
pattern
1882
Glass
Canton Glass Company,
Ohio
12 × 7⅛ × 7⅛ in.
(30.5 × 18.1 × 18.1cm)
Brooklyn Museum, Gift of
Mrs. William Greig Walker
by subscription, 40.225 a-b

86 "Jumbo Objects to Being
Put in Irons. McWhirter &
Wilson, Dry Goods, No. 165
Market St., Newark, N.J."
1882
Color lithograph trade card
J. H. Bufford's Sons, Boston
4½ × 2¾ in. (11.5 × 7 cm)

Somers Historical Society,
94.1.27

87 "Giving Jumbo a Friendly
Push Up Broadway, N.Y.,
U.S.A. Compliments of
Beatty."
1882
Color lithograph trade card
J. H. Bufford's Sons, Boston
4½ × 2¾ in. (11.5 × 7 cm)
Somers Historical Society,
94.1.27

88 "Jumbo Reaching for
Candy. McWhirter & Wilson,
Dry Goods, No. 165 Market
St., Newark, N.J."
ca. 1882
Color lithograph trade card
J. H. Bufford's Sons, Boston
4½ × 2¾ in. (11.5 × 7 cm)
Somers Historical Society,
94.1.27

89 "Jumbo Must Go,
Because Drawn by
Willimantic Thread!"
ca. 1882
Color lithograph trade card
Forbes Co., Boston
3⅜ × 5¾ in.
(8.6 × 14.7 cm)
Somers Historical Society,
94.1.27

90 "See What Can Be Done
With Willimantic Six Cord
Spool Cotton!"
ca. 1882
Color lithograph trade card
Forbes Co., Boston
3⅜ × 5¾ in.
(8.6 × 14.7 cm)
Somers Historical Society,
94.1.27

91 Souvenir cross-section of
Jumbo's tusk
1885
Ivory, ink
5¼ × 4½ × ¼ in.
(13.4 × 11.5 × 0.7 cm)
Circus World Museum,
CWi-2635
See cat. entry 15.

92 Jumbo the elephant
ca. 1885
Wool, linen
38½ × 39 in.
(97.8 × 99.1 cm)
Shelburne Museum,
Shelburne, Vermont, 9-M-5,
1954-604

93 Billstand for L. B. Lent's
New York Circus, Bangor,
Maine
1868

82

83

85

86

88

90

89

87

92

93

95

96

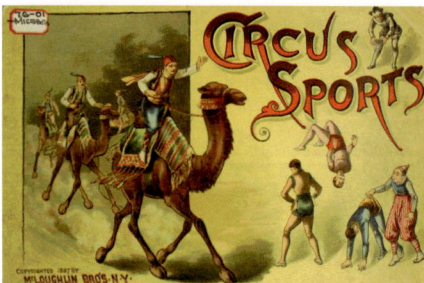

105

Stereographic photograph
3¼ × 6¾ in.
(8.3 × 17.2 cm)
Collection of Matthew
Wittmann

94 Interior view of Barnum's
Roman Hippodrome
1874
Stereographic photograph
E. & H. T. Anthony & Co.,
New York
4 × 7.1 in. (10 × 18 cm)
The John and Mable Ringling
Museum of Art, Tibbals
Collection, ht0005384
See cat. entry 12.

95 "Barnums Parade, N.Y."
ca. 1880
Stereographic photograph
E. & H. T. Anthony & Co.,
New York
3¼ × 6¾ in.
(8.3 × 17.2 cm)
Collection of Matthew
Wittmann

96 "Equestriennes"
1891
Color lithograph poster
United States Printing Co.,
Cincinnati
28 × 41½ in.
(71.2 × 105.5 cm)
Shelburne Museum,
Shelburne, Vermont, Gift of
Harry T. Peters Sr. Family,
1959, 1959-67.104

97 Strobridge Lithographing
Co. billstand on Madison
Square Garden, for "P. T.
Barnum & Co.'s Greatest
Show on Earth & the Great
London Circus Combined
with Sanger's Royal
British Menagerie & Grand
International Shows—Adam
Forepaugh's New and
Greatest All-Feature Show
without an Equal on Earth."
1887
Eleven albumen-print
panorama
9½ × 120 in.
(24.2 × 304.8 cm)
Circus World Museum
See fig. 3.22.

98 "The Barnum and Bailey
Greatest Show on Earth"
with female ringmaster,
clown, and rider
1897
Color lithograph poster
Strobridge Lithographing
Co., Cincinnati & New York
83½ × 40¼ in.
(212.1 × 102.3 cm)

The New-York Historical
Society
See cat. entry 18.

99 "The Barnum & Bailey
Greatest Show on Earth
/ The Terror of Forest and
Jungle / The Armored Indian
Rhinoceros"
1910
Color lithograph poster
Strobridge Lithographing
Co., Cincinnati & New York
83¼ × 40 in.
(211.5 × 101.6 cm)
Collection of The New-York
Historical Society, PR55-2
See fig. 3.24.

100 לאמפ
און זיין וואונדערבארעם
אלאדין (Aladdin and his
Wonderful Lamp)
1918
Illustrated poster with
Yiddish and English text
Fordinsky's Print, Brooklyn
17 × 12¼ in.
(43.2 × 31.2 cm)
Circus World Museum,
CWi-2307
See fig. 3.27.

101 "Ringling Bros and
Barnum & Bailey Combined
Shows" with springing tiger
Charles Livingston Bull
(1874–1932)
ca. 1920
Color lithograph poster
Strobridge Lithographing
Co., Cincinnati & New York
28¼ × 42¼ in.
(71.8 × 107.3 cm)
The John and Mable Ringling
Museum of Art, Tibbals
Collection, ht2001435
See fig. 3.21.

102 "Ringling Bros and
Barnum & Bailey / 'First and
Only Genuine Sacred White
Elephant Ever Permitted to
Leave His Native Land'"
1927
Color lithograph poster
Strobridge Lithographing
Co., Cincinnati & New York
83¼ × 40 in.
(211.5 × 101.6 cm)
New York State Museum,
Albany, H-1975.214.73
See cat. entry 23.

103 Performer's jacket
ca. 1830
Cotton and silk
Neck center to sleeve: 26 in.
(66.1 cm); width shoulder-
to-shoulder: 15 in. (38.1 cm)

Benjamin F. Brown
Collection, William L.
Clements Library, University
of Michigan; M-4067, Textile
Storage Box.
See cat. entry 3.

104 "The Boy Hero / Young
Clarence Palmer in His
Great Acts of Horsemanship
without Saddle or Bridle.
With Spalding & Rogers'
Two Circuses."
John H. Goater
1854
Lithograph
T. W. Strong, New York
23¼ × 17¾ in.
(59.1 × 45.1 cm)
The New-York Historical
Society, PR-055
See fig. 3.10.

105 *Circus Sports*
1887
Chromolithographed
picture book
McLoughlin Bros., New York
8 × 12 in. folded
(20.4 × 30.5 cm)
Brown University Library

106 A Peep at the Circus
Picture Puzzle
1887
Printed paper, cardboard
McLoughlin Bros., New York
12¼ × 10¼ × 2⅜ in.
(31 × 26 × 6 cm)
Courtesy of The Strong,
Rochester, New York,
107.4230
See fig. 3.11.

107 Fun at the Circus
1897
Board game in box
Printed paper, cardboard,
wood playing pieces, spinner
McLoughlin Bros., New York
Box: 17 × 17 × 1 in.
(43.2 × 43.2 × 2.5 cm)
Courtesy of The Strong,
Rochester, New York,
107.3861
See cat. entry 17.

108 Bandwagon from the
"Royal Circus"
ca. 1925
Painted sheet metal, cast
iron
Hubley Manufacturing Co.,
Lancaster, Penn.
10 × 29⅛ × 5¼ in.
(25.4 × 74 × 13.4 cm)
Courtesy of The Strong,
Rochester, New York,
77.2233

109 Monkey cage wagon from the "Royal Circus"
ca. 1925
Painted cast iron with glass
Hubley Manufacturing Co., Lancaster, Penn.
8⅛ × 12⅝ × 3⅜ in.
(20.5 × 32 × 8.5 cm)
Courtesy of The Strong, Rochester, New York,
107.3265

110 Giraffe cage wagon from the "Royal Circus"
ca. 1927
Painted cast iron, lead, tin plate
Hubley Manufacturing Co., Lancaster, Penn.
9 × 16½ × 4¾ in.
(23 × 42 × 12 cm)
Courtesy of The Strong, Rochester, New York,
79.515
See fig. 3.12.

111 Ring-a-Ling Circus
1925
Spring-wound mechanical figure
Pressed tin, lithographed
Louis Marx & Company, New York
7½ × 7¾ in. (19.2 × 19.7 cm)
Courtesy of The Strong, Rochester, New York,
74.563

112 *Lulu Lataska, Snake Charmer*
Charles Eisenmann (1850-1927?)
ca. 1885
Cabinet card, albumen print
6 × 4 in. (15.2 × 10.2 cm)
Ronald G. Becker Collection of Charles Eisenmann Photographs, Special Collections Research Center, Syracuse University Library, Syracuse, New York
See cat. entry 13.

113 *Mme. Fortune Clofullia, Bearded Lady*
Charles Eisenmann
(1850–1927?)
ca. 1885
Cabinet card, albumen print
6 × 4 in. (15.2 × 10.2 cm)
Ronald G. Becker Collection of Charles Eisenmann Photographs, Special Collections Research Center, Syracuse University Library, Syracuse, New York

114 *Jo Jo the Dog Faced Boy*
Charles Eisenmann

(1850–1927?)
ca. 1885
Cabinet card, albumen print
6 × 4 in. (15.2 × 10.2 cm)
Ronald G. Becker Collection of Charles Eisenmann Photographs, Special Collections Research Center, Syracuse University Library, Syracuse, New York
See cat. entry 13.

115 *Mr. I. W. Sprague, Human Skeleton*
Charles Eisenmann
(1850–1927?)
1883
Carte-de-visite, albumen print
3 × 2½ in. (7.6 × 6.4 cm)
Ronald G. Becker Collection of Charles Eisenmann Photographs, Special Collections Research Center, Syracuse University Library, Syracuse, New York
See cat. entry 13.

116 *Zulu Warriors, Princess & Child*
Charles Eisenmann
(1850–1927?)
ca. 1885
Cabinet card, albumen print
6 × 4 in. (15.2 × 10.2 cm)
Ronald G. Becker Collection of Charles Eisenmann Photographs, Special Collections Research Center, Syracuse University Library, Syracuse, New York
See cat. entry 13.

117 *Mr. and Mrs. M. V. Bates, Giants and Unidentified Man*
Charles Eisenmann
(1850–1927?)
ca. 1885
Cabinet card, albumen print
6 × 4 in. (15.2 × 10.2 cm)
Ronald G. Becker Collection of Charles Eisenmann Photographs, Special Collections Research Center, Syracuse University Library, Syracuse, New York

118 *Felix Wehrle, The Elastic Skin Man*
Charles Eisenmann
(1850–1927?)
ca. 1885
Cabinet card, albumen print
6 × 4 in. (15.2 × 10.2 cm)
Ronald G. Becker Collection of Charles Eisenmann Photographs, Special Collections Research Center, Syracuse University Library, Syracuse, New York

119 *The Australian Children, Pinheads*
Charles Eisenmann
(1850–1927?)
ca. 1885
Cabinet card, albumen print
6 × 4 in. (15.2 × 10.2 cm)
Ronald G. Becker Collection of Charles Eisenmann Photographs, Special Collections Research Center, Syracuse University Library, Syracuse, New York

120 *Laloo, Boy with Parasitic Twin*
Charles Eisenmann
(1850–1927?)
ca. 1885
Cabinet card, albumen print
6 × 4 in. (15.2 × 10.2 cm)
Ronald G. Becker Collection of Charles Eisenmann Photographs, Special Collections Research Center, Syracuse University Library, Syracuse, New York

121 *Anne E. Leak, Armless Wonder*
Charles Eisenmann
(1850–1927?)
ca. 1885
Cabinet card, albumen print
6 × 4 in. (15.2 × 10.2 cm)
Ronald G. Becker Collection of Charles Eisenmann Photographs, Special Collections Research Center, Syracuse University Library, Syracuse, New York
See fig. 3.14.

122 *Big Foot Ann, Elephantitis Feet*
Charles Eisenmann
(1850–1927?)
ca. 1885
Cabinet card, albumen print
6 × 4 in. (15.2 × 10.2 cm)
Ronald G. Becker Collection of Charles Eisenmann Photographs, Special Collections Research Center, Syracuse University Library, Syracuse, New York

123 *Millie - Christine, Siamese Twins*
Charles Eisenmann
(1850–1927?)
ca. 1885
Cabinet card, albumen print
6 × 4 in. (15.2 × 10.2 cm)
Ronald G. Becker Collection of Charles Eisenmann Photographs, Special Collections Research Center, Syracuse University Library, Syracuse, New York

108

110

111

113

119

117

120

118

122

123

HISTORY AND MEDICAL DESCRIPTION
OF THE
TWO-HEADED GIRL.

124

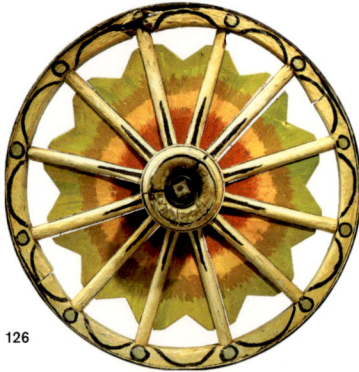

126

128

133

129

134

124 *History and Medical Description of the Two-Headed Girl*
1869
Pamphlet with woodcut illustrations
Engraved by Roylance & Purcell, New York; printed by Warren, Johnson & Co., Buffalo
7 × 5 in. (17.8 × 12.7 cm)
Shelburne Museum, Shelburne, Vermont, MS-398 Peters Ephemera B1F6

125 "Miss Louise and Her Den of Alligators."
Siegmund Bock (active early 20th century)
ca. 1915
Painted canvas
97 × 136½ in. (246.4 × 346.7 cm)
Circus World Museum, CWi-2654
See fig. 3.13.

126 Wagon wheel
late 19th century
Painted wood and metal
43 in. (109.3 cm) diameter
Somers Historical Society, 2005.68

127 Page figure from tableau cage wagon
Attributed to the workshop of Samuel Robb (1851–1928)
1882–83
Polychrome wood
59 × 15 × 12½ in. (149.9 × 38.1 × 31.8 cm)
Shelburne Museum, Shelburne, Vermont, 1954: FC 10
See fig. 3.19.

128 Design for the "Fairy Tales" tableau wagon
Attributed to Harry Ogden (1857–1936)
1902–3
Albumen print of original drawing
14¼ × 19⅜ in. (36.2 × 49.2 cm)
The New-York Historical Society.

129 Broom from the "Fairy Tales" tableau wagon
Workshop of Samuel Robb (1851–1928)
1902–3
Wood carving
90½ × 15¾ × 11 in. (229.9 × 40.1 × 28 cm)
Shelburne Museum,

Shelburne, Vermont, 27, FC-9

130 Design for the "Africa" tableau wagon
Attributed to Harry Ogden (1857–1936)
1902–3
Albumen print of original drawing
12¼ × 17 in. (31.1 × 43.2 cm)
The New-York Historical Society.
See cat. entry 19.

131 Sculpture of Europa, from "Africa" tableau wagon
1902–3
Wood carving
Workshop of Samuel Robb (1851–1928)
56 × 35 × 60 in. (142.3 × 88.9 × 152.4 cm)
From the Collections of The Henry Ford, Dearborn, Michigan, 31.815.1.3
See cat. entry 19.

132 Sculpture of Standing Warrior with Spear, from "Africa" tableau wagon
1902–3
Wood carving
Workshop of Samuel Robb (1851–1928)
69 × 18 × 16 × 67 in. (175.3 × 45.8 × 40.7 × 170.2 cm)
From the Collections of The Henry Ford, Dearborn, Michigan, 31.815.1.6
See cat. entry 19.

133 Model of the "Africa" tableau wagon
Roy Arnold
ca. 1950
Painted wood
15¾ × 67 × 9½ in. (40.1 × 170.2 x 24.2 cm)
Shelburne Museum, Shelburne, Vermont, 56.1.1

134 Sideshow band
Frederick Whitman Glasier (1866–1950)
ca. 1905, printed 2009
Print from a glass plate negative
26¼ × 32¼ in. (66.7 × 81.9 cm)
The John and Mable Ringling Museum of Art, Glasier Glass Plate Negative Collection, 0701

135 "The Great Hagenbeck-Wallace Circus / Seals That Exhibit Intelligence

Scarcely Less Than Human in Marvelously Skillful Performances."
1920
Color lithograph
Erie Lithograph & Printing Company, Erie, Penn.
40½ × 27½ in. (102.9 × 69.9 cm)
Shelburne Museum, Shelburne, Vermont, 27.4-515

136 "Ringling Bros Magnificent 1200 Character Spectacle / Joan of Arc"
1913
Color lithograph poster
Strobridge Lithographing Co., Cincinnati & New York
48⅝ × 39 in. (123.6 × 99.1 cm)
Shelburne Museum, Shelburne, Vermont, 27.4-512
See fig. 3.28.

137 Sword prop for circus spectacle
early 20th century
Metal
36½ × 4½ × ¾ in. (92.7 × 11.4 x 1.9 cm)
The John and Mable Ringling Museum of Art, Gift of Howard Tibbals, 2007, SN11160.2

138 Shield prop for circus spectacle
early 20th century
Metal
2 × 22 × 22 in. (5.1 × 55.9 × 55.9 cm)
The John and Mable Ringling Museum of Art, Gift of Howard Tibbals, 2007, SN11160.1

139 Horn prop for circus spectacle
early 20th century
Metal, leather
15 × 8½ × 5 in. (38.1 × 21.6 × 12.7 cm)
The John and Mable Ringling Museum of Art, Gift of Howard Tibbals, 2007, SN11160.3

140 Cast of Ringling Bros. Circus spectacle "Joan of Arc"
G. E. Palfrey
1912
Panoramic photograph
8 × 43 in. (20.4 × 109.3 cm)
Circus World Museum

4. SCENES FROM THE 20th CENTURY

141 Tiny Kline "slide for life" stunt, Times Square
1932
Film clip from *Gizmo!* (1977); directed by Howard Smith
High Wire Production
2 min.
Bard Graduate Center: Decorative Arts, Design History, Material Culture; New York

142 *The Lancer*
Walt Kuhn (1880–1949)
1939
Oil on canvas
45½ × 26¼ in.
(115.57 × 66.68 cm)
Currier Museum of Art, Manchester, New Hampshire. Museum Purchase: Currier Funds, 1958.7

143 *Three Ring Circus*
Milton Avery (1885–1965)
ca. 1939
Oil on canvas
32 × 48 in.
(81.28 × 121.92 cm)
Collection of AXA Equitable, New York
See fig. 4.9.

144 Ringling Bros. and Barnum & Bailey Circus clowns outside Madison Square Garden
Edward J. Kelty (1888–1967)
1924
Gelatin silver print
12 × 20 in.
(30.5 × 50.8 cm)
The John and Mable Ringling Museum of Art, Tibbals Collection, ht0004827
See cat. entry 22.

145 Ringling Bros. and Barnum & Bailey Circus sideshow performers in Madison Square Garden
Edward J. Kelty (1888–1967)
1928
Gelatin silver print
12 × 20 in.
(30.5 × 50.8 cm)
The John and Mable Ringling

Museum of Art, Tibbals Collection, ht0004828

146 Ringling Bros. and Barnum & Bailey Circus interior view of cast and audience at Madison Square Garden
Edward J. Kelty (1888–1967)
1932
Gelatin silver print
12 × 20 in.
(30.5 × 50.8 cm)
The John and Mable Ringling Museum of Art, Tibbals Collection, ht0004777
See cat. entry 22.

147 Ringling Bros. and Barnum & Bailey Circus interior view of cast and audience under canvas in Brooklyn
Edward J. Kelty (1888–1967)
1931
Gelatin silver print
12 × 20 in.
(30.5 × 50.8 cm)
The John and Mable Ringling Museum of Art, Tibbals Collection, ht0004809

148 "Cheerful Gardner and His Bulls / Hagenbeck-Wallace Circus—Yankee Stadium in Background. / June 22nd 1933"
Edward J. Kelty (1888–1967)
1933
Gelatin silver print
12 × 20 in.
(30.5 × 50.8 cm)
The John and Mable Ringling Museum of Art, Tibbals Collection, ht0005131
See fig. 4.3.

149 "Cole Bros.—Clyde Beatty Circus / New York Hippodrome—1937"
Edward J. Kelty (1888–1967)
1937
Gelatin silver print
12 × 20 in.
(30.5 × 50.8 cm)
The John and Mable Ringling Museum of Art, Tibbals Collection, ht0004976
See fig. 4.13.

150 WPA Circus personnel, in Brooklyn
ca. 1936
Gelatin silver print
16 × 19⅞ in.
(40.7 × 50.5 cm)

Prints & Photographs Division, Library of Congress, Washington, D.C.
See fig. 4.7.

151 Children at WPA Festival in Sheep Meadow, Central Park, May 2, 1936
Dick Rose
1936
Gelatin silver print
16 × 19⅞ in. (40.7 × 50.5 cm)
Prints & Photographs Division, Library of Congress, Washington, D.C.
See cat. entry 25.

152 "The World's Greatest Circus / Under the Big Tent… Schley Ave. at E. 177th St., Bronx…"
1936
Silkscreen poster
Poster Division, Federal Theatre, New York City
21⅞ × 13¾ in.
(55.6 × 35 cm)
Music Division, Library of Congress, Washington, D.C.
See fig. 4.6.

153 "The Worlds Greatest Circus… 202 St. & Hollis Ave. Hollis L.I…"
1937
Silkscreen poster
Poster Division, Federal

Theatre, New York City
22 × 14 in.
(55.9 × 35.6 cm)
Music Division, Library of Congress, Washington, D.C.

154 "Children's Circus Rebate Tickets / Free / Ask for Them Inside"
ca. 1935
Silkscreen poster
Poster Division, Federal Theatre, New York City
11 × 14 in. (28 × 35.6 cm)
Music Division, Library of Congress, Washington, D.C.
See cat. entry 25.

155 *W.P.A. Circus*
William Hicks (b. 1895)
ca. 1937
Etching, aquatint
14½ × 11 in.
(36.8 × 28 cm)
Spencer Museum of Art,

135

142

137

139

138

140

145

147

153

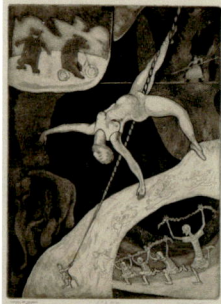

155

156

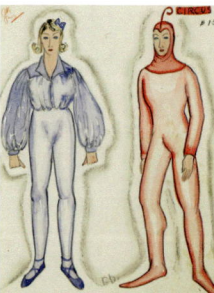

157

158

159

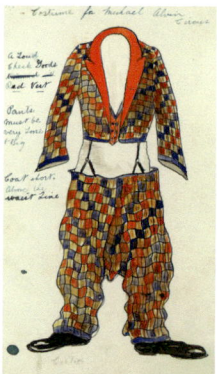

160

161

The University of Kansas,
Gift of the W.P.A Arts
Project, 0000.0365

156 Costume design for
Mrs. Franklin
Robert Byrne
ca. 1936
Ink, watercolor, and pastel,
on paper
11⅞ × 8⅞ in.
(30.2 × 22.6 cm)
Music Division, Library of
Congress, Washington, D.C.

157 Costume designs for
Marie Genaro and Albert
Arden
Robert Byrne
ca. 1936
Ink, watercolor, and pastel,
on paper
10 × 8 in. (25.4 × 20.4 cm)
Music Division, Library of
Congress, Washington, D.C.

158 Costume design for
the Flying Russells
Robert Byrne
ca. 1936
Ink, watercolor, and pastel,
on paper
10 × 8 in. (25.4 × 20.4 cm)
Music Division, Library of
Congress, Washington, D.C.

159 Costume design for
Michael Alvin
Robert Byrne
ca. 1936
Ink, watercolor, and pastel,
on paper
10 × 6 in.
(25.4 × 15.3 cm)
Music Division, Library of
Congress, Washington, D.C.

160 Costume designs for
Minnie and Bill
Robert Byrne
ca. 1936
Ink, watercolor, and pastel,
on paper
11⅞ × 9 in.
(30.2 × 22.9 cm)
Music Division, Library of
Congress, Washington, D.C.

161 Horse stand
mid-20th century
Painted wood
12 × 19½ × 19½ in.
(30.5 × 49.6 × 49.6 cm)
New York State Museum,
Albany, H-1982.199.3

162 Sleeping at the circus,
Madison Square Garden,
New York
Weegee (1899–1968)

June 28, 1943
Gelatin silver print
10⅜ × 13⅝ in.
(26.4 × 34.6 cm)
International Center of
Photography, New York,
Bequest of Wilma Wilcox,
1993 (2367.1993)
See cat. entry 27.

163 "Resourceful girl
manages to watch a man on
flying trapeze and feed hot
dog to escort at same time."
Weegee (1899–1968)
April 18, 1943
Gelatin silver print
7¾ × 9⅝ in.
(19.7 × 24.4 cm)
International Center of
Photography, New York,
Bequest of Wilma Wilcox,
1993 (7921.1993)
See cat. entry 27.

164 "'Spangles,' the
new Ringling Brothers
Continental Circus, has the
dazzling aerial acts of the
old show, as these upturned
faces in the audience testify."
Weegee (1899–1968)
June 18, 1943
Gelatin silver print
10⅝ × 12½ in.
(27 × 31.8 cm)
International Center of
Photography, New York,
Bequest of Wilma Wilcox,
1993 (7959.1993)
See cat. entry 27.

165 Circus audience,
New York
Weegee (1899–1968)
ca. 1943
Gelatin silver print
9¼ × 7½ in.
(23.5 × 19.1 cm)
International Center of
Photography, New York,
Bequest of Wilma Wilcox,
1993 (7979.1993)
See cat. entry 27.

166 Circus audience,
New York
Weegee (1899–1968)
ca. 1943
Gelatin silver print
9½ × 7⅝ in.
(24.1 × 19.4 cm)
International Center of
Photography, New York,
Bequest of Wilma Wilcox,
1993 (7998.1993)

167 Circus audience,
New York
Weegee (1899–1968)

Gelatin silver print
ca. 1943
7⅝ × 9½ in.
(19.4 × 24.1 cm)
International Center of
Photography, New York,
Bequest of Wilma Wilcox,
1993 (8003.1993)

168 Circus audience,
New York
Weegee (1899–1968)
ca. 1943
Gelatin silver print
7⅝ × 9½ in.
(19.4 × 24.1 cm)
International Center of
Photography, New York,
Bequest of Wilma Wilcox,
1993 (8005.1993)

169 *Spectators*,
New York
Weegee (1899–1968)
ca. 1953
Gelatin silver print
7⅞ × 9¾ in.
(20 × 24.8 cm)
International Center of
Photography, New York,
Bequest of Wilma Wilcox,
1993 (8028.1993)

170 Circus audience,
New York
Weegee (1899–1968)
ca. 1943
Gelatin silver print
10 × 13⅜ in.
(25.4 × 34 cm)
International Center of
Photography, New York,
Bequest of Wilma Wilcox,
1993 (7982.1993)

171 "Ringling Bros and
Barnum & Bailey Circus
/ The Greatest Show on
Earth" with Kitty Clark and
elephant
George Howe (1886–
1955), Studio of Norman
Bel Geddes
ca. 1945
Color lithograph poster
McCandlish Lithograph
Corp., Philadelphia
42 × 28 in.
(106.7 × 71.2 cm)
Collection of Matthew
Wittmann
See cat. entry 26.

172 "Ringling Bros / Barnum
& Bailey" with monkey band
Lawson Wood (1878–1957)
1943
Color lithograph poster
26 × 39¾ in.
(66.1 × 101 cm)

Shelburne Museum, Shelburne, Vermont, Gift of Harry T. Peters Sr. Family, 1959, 27.4-415
See fig. 4.10.

173 "Ringling Bros and Barnum & Bailey Circus" with leopard head
Studio of Norman Bel Geddes
1956
Color lithograph poster
Strobridge Lithographing Co., Cincinnati & New York
51 × 29 in.
(129.6 × 73.7 cm)
New York State Museum, Albany

174 *Ringling Bros. and Barnum & Bailey Circus Parade*
William Day
1945
Digital copy of 16mm color film
2 min.
Collection of Robert F. Sabia

175 "Ringling Bros and Barnum & Bailey Presents Old King Cole and Mother Goose"
George Howe (1886–1955), Studio of Norman Bel Geddes
1941
Color lithograph poster
McCandlish Lithograph Corp., Philadelphia
41½ × 27½ in.
(105.4 × 69.9 cm)
The John and Mable Ringling Museum of Art, Tibbals Collection, ht2001695
See cat. entry 26.

176 *Ringling Bros—Barnum & Bailey Circus Magazine 1942 / Featuring Peter Arno's Original Circus Drawings*
1942
Ink on paper
Circus Publishing Co.
11¼ × 8½ in.
(28.6 × 21.6 cm)
Collection of Matthew Wittmann
See chronology, fig. C.16.

177 "Mama's in the Park" costume design
Miles White (1914–2000)
1955
Paint and pencil on paper
12 × 10 in. (30.5 × 25.4 cm)
The John and Mable Ringling Museum of Art, Tibbals

Collection, ht300748
See cat. entry 31.

178 "Mama's in the Park" bodice and skirt costume
Designed by Miles White (1914–2000), from the studio of Max Weldy
1955
Velvet, sequins
60 × 30 × 30 in.
(152.4 × 76.2 × 76.2 cm)
The John and Mable Ringling Museum of Art, Gift of Max Weldy and Ringling Bros. and Barnum & Bailey Circus, SN1562.706.66a-b

179 "Rainbow Round the World" clown costume design
Miles White (1914–2000)
1955
Paint and ink on paper
12 × 10 in.
(30.5 × 25.4 cm)
The John and Mable Ringling Museum of Art, Tibbals Collection, ht300751
See fig. 4.14.

180 "Rainbow Round the World" clown costume
Designed by Miles White (1914–2000), from the studio of Max Weldy
1955
Felt and sequins
35 × 30 in.
(88.9 × 76.2 cm)
The John and Mable Ringling Museum of Art, Gift of Max Weldy and Ringling Bros. and Barnum & Bailey Circus, SN1562.705.2a-b
See fig. 4.15.

181 "Rainbow Round the World" mermaid costume design
Miles White (1914–2000)
1955
Paint and ink on paper
20 × 18 in.
(50.8 × 45.7 cm)
The John and Mable Ringling Museum of Art, Tibbals Collection, ht3000788

182 Friede DeMarlo frog head
ca. 1910
Papier mâché, paint, cotton, and sequins
14 × 14½ × 13½ in.
(35.6 × 36.9 × 34.3 cm)
New York State Museum, Albany, 7-18-3, H-1987.61.1
See cat. entry 21.

183 Friede DeMarlo frog costume
ca. 1910
Cotton and silk trim with spangles
30 × 40 in.
(76.2 × 101.6 cm)
New York State Museum, Albany, 7-18-3, H-1987.62.430

184 *Friede De Marlo, The Original Frog Lady*
ca. 1910
Hand-colored albumen print photograph
7¾ × 5⅞ in.
(19.69 × 15 cm)
New York State Museum, Albany
See cat. entry 21.

185 "La Marletta Presenting Her Wonderful Combination Act A Symphony in the Air… De Marlo in His Trapeze Offering The Laughing Mephistopheles"
ca. 1925
Poster
14 × 10 in.
(35.6 × 25.4 cm)
New York State Museum, Albany
See cat. entry 21.

186 Harry DeMarlo Mephistopheles costume
ca. 1920
Wool knit, silk trim, and sequins
Chest: 46 × 32 in.
(116.9 × 81.3 cm)
New York State Museum, Albany, H-1987.61.4
See cat. entry 21.

187 DeMarlo's trapeze bar
ca. 1920
Metal, rope
85 × 41½ × 3 in.
(216 × 105.5 × 7.7 cm)
New York State Museum, Albany, H-1987.62.719

188 Friede DeMarlo iron jaw apparatus
ca. 1925
Metal, leather
25 × 2½ × 2¼ in.
(63.5 × 6.4 × 5.7 cm)
New York State Museum, Albany, H-1987.62.724

189 De Marlo performing-dog costume
ca. 1925
Rayon knit and sequins
8 × 28 × 14¾ in.
(20.4 × 71.2 × 37.5 cm)

166

167

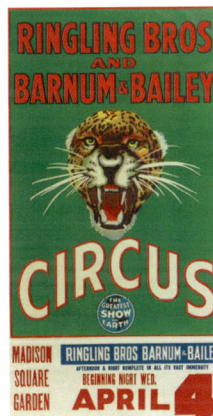

168

169

170

173

181

178

183

187

188

189

191

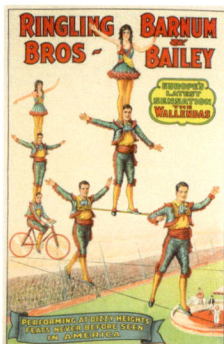

192

201

194

198

New York State Museum, Albany, H-1987.62.431

190 *May Wirth*
Harry Atwell (1879–1957)
ca. 1920
Inscription: "Best wishes from May Wirth"
Gelatin silver print
8 × 10 in. (20.3 × 25.4 cm)
The John and Mable Ringling Museum of Art, Tibbals Collection, ht0004443
See chronology, fig. C.13.

191 "Ringling Bros and Barnum & Bailey Combined Shows / May Wirth The Greatest Bareback Rider of All Time"
ca. 1920
Color lithograph poster
Strobridge Lithographing Co., Cincinnati & New York
42¼ × 28 in.
(107.3 × 71.1 cm)
The John and Mable Ringling Museum of Art, Tibbals Collection, ht2001475

192 "Ringling Bros-Barnum & Bailey / Europe's Latest Sensation The Wallendas"
ca. 1928
Color lithograph poster
Erie Lithograph & Printing Company, Erie, Penn.
42 × 28 in.
(106.7 × 71.2 cm)
Shelburne Museum, Shelburne, Vermont, Gift of Harry T. Peters Sr. Family, 1959, 1959-67.194

193 *The Wallendas, New York*
Lisette Model (1901–1983)
1945
Gelatin silver print on board
23¾ × 19 in.
(60.3 × 48.3 cm)
International Center of Photography, Gift of Lisette Model Foundation in memory of Joseph G. Blum, 1993 (106.1993)
See cat. entry 30.

194 Karl Wallenda pants, shirt, and vest
ca. 1955
Satin, cotton gabardine, sequins
Shirt: 30 × 20 in. (76.2 × 50.8 cm); vest 14 × 17 in. (35.6 × 43.2 cm); pants 40 × 16 in. (101.6 × 40.6 cm)
Wallenda family
The John and Mable Ringling Museum of Art, Gift of circus

fans from Showfolks Tent #122, SN1186.a-c

195 "Ringling Bros and Barnum & Bailey / The Human Projectile Hugo Zacchini… The Sensation of the Century!"
1929
Color lithograph poster
27½ × 35½ in.
(69.9 × 90.2 cm)
Illinois Lithograph Co.
Shelburne Museum, Shelburne, Vermont, Gift of Harry T. Peters Sr. Family, 1959, 1959–67.303
See cat. entry 24.

196 "Hugo Zacchini— Human Projectile / Ringling Brothers and Barnum & Bailey Combined Circus / Brooklyn, N.Y. May 19th 1933"
Edward J. Kelty (1888–1967)
1933
Gelatin silver print
12 × 20 in.
(30.5 × 50.8 cm)
The John and Mable Ringling Museum of Art, Tibbals Collection, ht0005012
See cat. entry 24.

197 "Hagenbeck-Wallace Trained Wild Animal Circus / Clyde Beatty the Jungle King in a Single-Handed Battle with 40 of the Most Ferocious Brutes that Breathe!"
ca. 1934
Color lithograph poster
Erie Lithograph & Printing Company, Erie, Penn.
20¼ × 28 in.
(51.4 × 71.1 cm)
The John and Mable Ringling Museum of Art, Tibbals Collection, ht2000830
See cat. entry 29.

198 Clyde Beatty at Madison Square Garden
Edward J. Kelty (1888–1967)
1934
Gelatin silver print
12 × 20 in.
(30.5 × 50.8 cm)
The John and Mable Ringling Museum of Art Archive, CM20015

199 Clyde Beatty pith helmet
ca. 1940
Pith
Label: "Genuine Pith Helmet

made in India expressly for Bailey of California"
13½ × 10¼ × 7 in.
(34.3 × 26.1 × 17.8 cm)
Circus World Museum, CWi-2643
See cat. entry 29.

200 Clyde Beatty whip
ca. 1940
Leather
11¾ × 15 × 1 in.
(29.9 × 38.1 × 2.6 cm)
Circus World Museum, CWi-2650
See cat. entry 29.

201 Clyde Beatty chair
ca. 1940
Wood
16 × 16 × 35 in.
(40.7 × 40.7 × 88.9 cm)
Circus World Museum, CWi-2644

202 Clyde Beatty shirt and jodhpurs
ca. 1940
Cotton drilling
Shirt: 31 × 35 in. (78.8 × 88.9 cm); jodhpurs 40 × 15 in. (101.6 × 38.1 cm)
Circus World Museum, CWi-2649

203 Al Langdon jacket
ca. 1920
Wool, gold braid, metal buttons
Label: "DeMoulin Bros. & Co., Grenville, IL"
32 × 18 in.
(81.3 × 45.8 cm)
Circus World Museum, CWi-2637

204 Elephant stand
mid-20th century
Painted metal
19 × 32 × 32 in.
(48.3 × 81.3 × 81.3 cm)
New York State Museum, Albany, H-1982.199.2

205 "Ringling Bros and Barnum & Bailey Circus / The Greatest Show on Earth" with Felix Adler
George Howe (1886–1955)
1943
Color lithograph poster
McCandlish Lithograph Corp., Philadelphia
21 × 28 in.
(53.3 × 71.1 cm)
The John and Mable Ringling Museum of Art, Tibbals Collection, ht2001715
See cat. entry 28.

206 Felix Adler clown suit
ca. 1950
Cotton
55 × 22 in.
(139.7 × 55.9 cm)
Circus World Museum,
CWi-2645

207 Felix Adler clown shoes
ca. 1950
Leather
19 × 10 × 10 in.
(48.3 × 25.4 × 25.4 cm)
Circus World Museum,
CWi-2653
See cat. entry 28.

208 Felix Adler birdcage hat
ca. 1950
Mixed media
9 × 9 × 12 in.
(22.9 × 22.9 × 30.5 cm)
Circus World Museum,
CWi-2647
See page 6.

209 Felix Adler bowtie
ca. 1940
Cardboard, cotton, costume
jewelry
19½ × 7½ in.
(49.6 × 19.1 cm)
Circus World Museum,
CWi-2628

210 Merle Evans band
uniform
ca.1955
Wool, gold embroidery,
metal buttons
Label: "A. Dubois of New
York City"
Jacket: 35 × 46 in. (88.9 ×
116.9 cm); pants 45¼ × 40
in. (115 × 101.6 cm); hat
4½ × 10½ × 11 in. (11.5 ×
26.7 × 28 cm)
New York State Museum,
Albany, H-1988.59.1 a-d
See cat. entry 32.

211 Merle Evans cornet
ca. 1955
Silvered brass
7 × 13 × 5 in.
(17.8 × 33.1 × 12.7 cm)
New York State Museum,
Albany, H-1977.165.309

212 "New Madison Square
Garden—Season 1926—
Ringling Brothers and
Barnum & Bailey Concert
Band.—Merle Evans, Band
Master."
Edward J. Kelty
(1888–1967)
1926
Gelatin silver print
12 × 20 in.

(30.5 × 50.8 cm)
The John and Mable Ringling
Museum of Art, Tibbals
Collection, ht0004850
See cat. entry 32.

213 Circus Time
Ringling Bros and Barnum
& Bailey Circus Band: Merle
Evans, Conductor
1953
Vinyl LP record
Decca Records
10.625 × 10.5 in.
(27 × 26.7 cm)
Shelburne Museum,
Shelburne, Vermont.
See cat. entry 32.

214 "New York School for
Circus Arts Presents the
Big Apple Circus"
Louisa Chase
1977
Cut paper
29 × 23 in.
(73.7 × 58.5 cm)
Big Apple Circus

215 Big Apple Circus
Nigel Nobel, director;
Frank Doelger and Howard
Meltzer, producers
1991
Film
27 min.
Home Box Office, New York
Big Apple Circus

216 "Clown About Town"
set design model
Daniel J. Kuchar
2000
Mixed media
20 × 20 × 20 in.
(50.8 × 50.8 × 50.8 cm)
Big Apple Circus

217 Barry Lubin "Grandma"
clown costume – wig, pearl
necklace, dress, bloomers,
socks, shows, purse
Roberta Lubin
2012
Mixed media
56 × 48 in.
(142.3 × 122 cm)
Big Apple Circus
See chronology, fig. C.22.

203

210

204

211

206

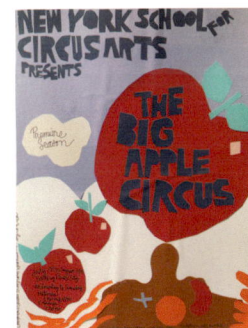

214

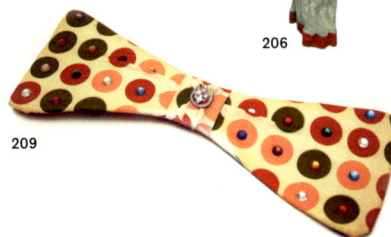

209

216

"It is the genius of the circus to give too much of everything."
—Brooks Atkinson, 1942

Appendix

The Knickerbocker 13, no. 1 (January 1839), 67–76.

CIRCUS.

'Unrivalled attraction! grand entrée! feats of the ring! ground and lofty tumbling! still vaulting by the whole company![']

I know of some villages, which are happy in an unusual seclusion, whose situation protects them from the intrusion of the world. So surrounded are they by hills, and so embosomed in forests, so 'remote from cities,' and from public highways, that the heart of Zimmerman might envy their solitude. The most violent tempests in the political world can hardly affect them. They are like mountains whose summits are basking in the sunbeams, while their base is uprooted by the storm. 'The wind and the hurricane rage in the distance; the destruction is beyond their horizon of peace.'

Thither, by the eternal impediments of nature, no post-routes or rail-ways can ever come, to work out their magical changes; no manufactories stun with their clatter, or darken the atmosphere with smoke. The spirit of utility, which is abroad in the country, which levels to the earth so many monuments of affection, and forbids any thing to stand as it is, cannot come *here*. There are few changes except the ever-recurring ones of nature and mortality. The aspect of to-day remains the same to-morrow; and the solitary spire which pierces the blue skies now, will fifty years hence look down upon the peaceful abodes of men 'whose fathers worshipped in this mountain.'

The primeval silence of these places remains almost unbroken; scarcely is echo awakened among the rocks. Their situation is not marked upon the maps, and their existence is a secret to the world. Perhaps a few quiet gentlemen come there in the summer, to sail on the clear lakes, or drop their lines for the golden-speckled trout. But they are wily fishermen; and when

'The melancholy days return, the saddest of the year,'

and they go back to the marts of commerce, careful are they not to reveal the pleasant spots where they laid in wait for the 'scaly people.'

One might suppose that the current of life ran along almost too sleepily, and that the inhabitants of such places would be ready to die with weariness and disgust. But let it be remembered, that they do not live in idleness, nor are their sickly natures fed with excitement, as a food. They have sports and pastimes in abundance, and incidents which the bustling world would deem unworthy of notice are continually occurring, to relieve them from monotony, and to create a spicy variety of life. Sometimes a pedlar comes along, and is a welcome visiter. He opens doors without knocking, and enters with the familiarity of a friend. His variegated wares are spread out; brass buttons, and tortoise-shell combs, and suspenders, and ear-rings, and jewelry of pure gold. The housewives find it to their advantage to purchase his salves and essences, and his o-*pod*-eldoc, as he terms it, which is a 'sartin cure for the rhumatiz.'

Ever and anon, there is a show of dancing puppets, and a barrel-organ turned by some worn-out soldier, whose simple airs a fat, rosy-faced woman accompanies, while in a very sweet voice, but a raw accent, she sings, rolling her dark, supplicating eyes to the windows:

'I'd be a butterfly, born in a bow'r,
Where roses and lilies and violets meet,
Roving for ever from flower to flower,
Kissing all things that is pretty, a-n-d sweet.
I'd never languish for wealth or for power,
I'd never sigh to see slaves at my feet.'

And not in vain does she expend her melody. For soon her eyes are refreshed by a pattering shower of silver coin, which honest boys collect from the earth, and place in her hands, while some kindhearted spirit crowns the whole with a goblet of sparkling water. She inhales the draught, more delicious than wine of the old vintage, and passes on to the next cottage, leaving a God's blessing, sweet to the rustic ear as the lately-expired music. A few moments elapse, and her distant voice is again heard; for having detected in a window a golden-haired, beautiful girl, peeping from behind the jalousies of the honeysuckle, she sings of the 'minstrel's return,' or of a youth now far, far away, but whom at midsummer the propitious fates will restore to the embrace of his mistress. And again, in a song not excelled for a simplicity which touches the heart, she declares the enduring attachments of home:

'Midst pleasures and palaces though I may roam,
Be it ever so humble, there's no place like home.'

I charge all persons, and especially husbandmen, that they reward most generously these only relics of the troubadours. Many a weary mile do they walk, the messengers of music. Small is the boon which they ask or desire, and entirely unequal to their deserts. Treat them kindly, treat them tenderly, and they will repay you ten-fold; neglect them, and the doric muse has perished.

There are few wandering fortune-tellers in the country, nor are our villages rendered animate by the scene of a gipsey encampment. Let those arrant poachers remain in England; their absence is certainly to be regretted, on the score of the picturesque. Yet we cannot accord with the solemn exclamation of the nursery song:

> 'Lo! mother Shipton and her cat
> Quite full of conjuration;
> And if more conjurers could be found,
> 'T were better for the nation.'

A travelling caravan is an integral portion of the great institute in the metropolis. When the summer comes, it is broken up into parts, which are dispersed in every section of the country, that the imprisoned beasts may have the benefit of pure air. These consist, for the most part, of a lion, a tiger, a black bear, a camel, a wild cat, a hyena, some torpid snakes, coiled up in a box, and in a separate apartment a panorama, and a man who 'sings Jim Crow.' This latter is the most noxious beast of the whole clan. Beside these, a great number of monkeys, apes, and ring-tailed babboons, are shut up in a community. These be capital fellows, full of spirits, which go the whole length of their ropes, and are better worth seeing, the spectators themselves being judges, than all the tigers, zebras, and hump-back camels, put together. Among themselves, they are' hale fellows,' chattering and grinning, jibing, and cracking their jokes, as if in some forest of Africa, save when a by-stander rolls in an 'apple of discord,' or a cake, and then the big ones flog the small ones unmercifully; and herein consists the kernel of the joke. A Shetland pony goes round and round in a circle, surmounted by a jocko in scarlet uniform, who proves himself an indomitable horseman. He leaps on and off, handles the reins with address, and cracks his whip like a Jehu. Sometimes a small African elephant is made to kneel down, and receive a tower on his shoulders. Those of the company who desire to ride, are requested to step forward, 'ladies first, gentlemen after-*wards*.' After a deal of hesitation, a servant-maid gathers courage, and simpering and dimpling, ambles into the arena. Her the showman politely assists to ascend. Another follows, and another, until all the seats are taken up. Then the beast moves once around, with his slow and heavy tramp, the *ladies* descend from their airy height, and are able to go home and say that they have ' ridden on the elephant.' Last of all, a negro is encouraged to mount the animal's bare back, and broadly grinning, is looking down upon the crowd below, when the latter, being privy to a joke, gives a violent shrug, and hurls him, as from a terrific

precipice, to the ground.

The menagerie is a very popular entertainment, unexceptionable on the score of morals, and visited by the 'most straitest sects' of the people. Do you see that tall, thin, straight, bony, green-spectacled man, who pries curiously into all the cages, and shuts up like a jack-knife when he bends? That is Mr. Simpson. He is a judge of these things, and has a collection at home; an ostrich's egg, a stuffed partridge, and some bugs in a bottle of spirits. He is followed by the lady superior of the female seminary, and a score of pupils, that they may lose none of his valuable remarks.

'Aha!' quoth he, 'here we have the lion, most properly denominated the king of beasts. He is a native of Africa, fierce in his might and terrible in his strength. Mark his flowing mane, his majestic port, his flaming eyes—his—his—his—*tail*. When he roars, heaven shakes, earth quakes, and hell trembles. Here, keeper, please be so good as make this lion roar.'

'Oh! no, no, no!' shriek a dozen voices, hysterically, 'don't let him roar!—do n't let him roar!'

'Well, well, as you please,' quoth Mr. Simpson, good-humoredly winking at madam.

'Here is the Jackal, who purwides food for the lion; a miserable sycophant and panderer for a king. Mark his mean aspect, and dirty appearance. He is emblematic of man. Alas! there *is* jackals in the world; jackals literary and jackals political.'

It is a season of still deeper excitement, in such a retired country village, when once a year, after several days' heralding, a train of great red wagons is seen approaching, marked in large letters, CIRCUS, 1, 2, 3, 4, and so on. This arrival has been talked of, and produces an immediate bustle and sensation. Fifty boys breaking loose from school, rush immediately to the street, and in treble tones cry 'Circus!' The ploughman lets his plough stand in the middle of the field, and leans over the fence. The blacksmith withdraws his brawny arm from the anvil, and stands in the door of his smithy. A man in the act of shaving, comes out with his face lathered, and a towel under his chin. The old woman who is washing in the porch, takes her dripping and smoking fingers from the Suds, peers over her spectacles, opens her mouth, and utters an ejaculation. The milkmaid leaves her pail to be kicked over by the cow. A wise-looking clerk puts his head out of

the window, with a pen stuck in his ear. A cat on the eaves of a house likewise looks down. The mother runs to call Johnny, who is playing in the yard, quick—quick—quick! before the procession moves by. He is too late. Ba-a-a-a! An invalid in bed leaps up, thinks he feels better, and shall be 'abundantly able to go.'

Meantime the cavalcade halts before the inn. The crowd closes in at once, to feast their eyes on the luggage, and see the company unpack. The spirited horses, perspiring with the long journey, stamp impatiently on the ground. The *corps* are a little out of patience, and annoyed by the crowd. A child gets under the horses' heels, and is dragged out by the hair of his head, unhurt. What rough-spoken, ill-looking fellows are the equestrians! How strangely will they be metamorphosed in a few hours—bright, dazzling, tricked out in gay attire, full of beautiful spangles! They are not themselves now; they are *acting* the difficult parts of every-day men. At night they will fall readily into their own characters, clowns, harlequins, and the most amusing fools in the world.

'May I be I there to see!'

Rapidly the intelligence of their arrival spreads into the adjacent country. The whole community are on the *qui vive*. There are uneasiness, anticipation, excitement. The village belles layout their trinkets, ornaments, and brightest calicoes, to adorn the boxes; the plough-boy scrapes his pence together, desperately determined on a standing in the pit. A discussion waxes warm among the graver part of the community, about the lawfulness of these amusements. Some of the young are troubled with doubts. The old people hesitate, demur, and at last give their consent. They have been once young themselves—such opportunities do not occur every day. Indeed it would be very difficult for anyone to demur, after reading the 'bill of fare,' a great blanket sheet, full of wood cuts and pictures; horses on the full run, and men bent into all possible shapes and contortions. 'Unrivalled Attraction! Grand entrée. Four-and-twenty Arabian horses. Celebrated equestrian Mr. Burke. Feats in the ring. Grand leap. Cups and ball. The entertainments to conclude with the laughable farce of Billy Button, or the Hunted Tailor.' As the hired man reads over this tempting bill, or failing to read, interprets the hieroglyphics, his mouth waters. '*I must go*!'—and he adds, resolutely clenching his teeth, '*I will go*.'

In the course of the day the equestrians have wrought industriously, and raised their white pavilion. It stands out on the green, in beautiful proportions, erected suddenly, as if by magic. A flag floats over its summit, on whose ample folds is inscribed ' Circus.' All things are ready for the evening's sport, and a death-like silence reigns over the village.

Who is he that walketh pensively in yonder green, beneath the shadow of the trees, with head bowed down, as if in thought, and plucking a leaf to pieces? It is the amiable minister of the parish. He is sore grieved in spirit. Hitherto has he led his flock without contradiction, conducting them safely through thorny places, and shielding them from the inclemency of the storm. And now forsooth the very devil has come to take them by force of arms. From his heart he regrets it. He has prayed over it, and wept over it, and slept over it, and dreamed of it. He has summoned a conclave of the principal men, remonstrated with the authorities of the town, and held up the whole thing in the length and breadth of its enormity. But the perverse men will heed none of his counsels or reproofs. He preached a sermon on the Sunday previous, in which he alarmed the young, and denounced in the most terrible terms all who should hold communion with Belial. He shed tears over the disregard of his reckless auditors. But there is mixed up with genuine grief a little vexation, because he cannot have his own way. If they will heed none of his counsel, if they will persist in their own downward course, he can but depart from them; he can but shake off the dust of his feet, and leave them to perish in their misdoings.

It is very hard to draw the line accurately betwixt virtue and vice, and it may be safer to err upon the right side. Yet there is a time for every thing. We cannot always be serious. The mind must have its carnival. We must crack the nuts of folly. To become a fool once a year, is a mark of wisdom; to be a perpetual fool, is beyond endurance. The gradual accumulation of spirits in the dullest person, will at length reach a height when it demands an exit.

'Qua data porta ruit.'*

What signifies it, whether it be let off in a round explosion, or hiss away at intervals, like steam. Talk not of mingling the useful with the sweet. We sometimes require folly without mixture—pure, unalloyed, unmitigated and concentrated folly. It is good to be attacked, to be sick, and to die with agonies of laughter. The storm of the passions purifies the atmosphere of the temper. With how much keener zest do we return to substantial pleasures, even as the sick man awakens to the deliciousness of health! Govern then your own conduct by the most rigid maxims, but beware how you denounce too bitterly, or condemn too terribly, unless yourselves are immaculate. Consistency is a most precious jewel. If you deem it a credit to abstain from trifles, indulging unreservedly in what is infinitely worse—if you cherish envy, or pride, or jealousy in the heart—if you sully by detraction the fair name of your neighbor, whom you are commanded to love as yourself—then certainly you 'strain at a gnat and swallow a camel.' To do these things, and without compunction, may be esteemed a more palpable dereliction, than to laugh at the antics of a tumbler or a clown. The voiceless eloquence of a good example persuades the young to virtue, but the harsher precepts of a rigorous code, will be more apt to compel them to a vagabond life.

The sun is just resting on the borders of the horizon, and making the summer evening lovely, when the whole equestrian *corps*, a signal being given, sally forth and wind through the grass-skirted lanes of the village. A band of music goes before, drawn in a chariot by four dappled horses. The notes of the bugle floating exquisitely on the tranquil air, fill the rustic bosom with enthusiasm. The equestrians follow in gorgeous, spangled dresses, the clown standing up on one leg, with a straw in his mouth, and giving a foretaste of those facetious inanities which he will exhibit at even. Just at dusk, they return to the pavilion. A motley crowd rushes hurriedly through the streets. The minister of the parish looks out from his window, and weeps. He is a good man, and God will shelter his little flock from harm. The scrupulous and the wavering are now decided. Those who but yesterday said, crabbedly, that they had 'no time, nor money nother, for such wild doings,' bustle off, 'just to see what's going on.' Many persons of approved gravity attend, who 'suld have known better.' To the negro population, the occasion is a heyday and holiday. The Pompeys are there, and the Catos are there, and the noble lineage of the Caesars. Thus all the population are collected beneath the great tent. No; there are a few unhappy boys without, who peep hopelessly through the crevices of the awning, but whom the door-keeper will soon discover, and send harshly away.

Just at this juncture, the gentleman who lives in the white cottage by the hill-side, and who has acted for a long time past in a very remarkable manner, having little intercourse with the neighbors, declining to answer questions, or to have his affairs inquired into, (he is either crazy or in love,) passes by that way, and thrusting his hand in his pocket, presents the lads a shilling each. Smiles and gratitude reward him.

The area of the enclosure is divided into the ring, pit, and boxes. A circular wooden frame-work depends in the centre, containing a great many tarnished lamps, and magniloquently called a chandelier. 'Splendid!' whispers the crowd. Let us inspect the company a few minutes, before the performances commence. The circular seats are crowded to the very roof. Behold there the bloom and flower of the country—the daughters of stout yeomen, brought hither by the beaux to view this rare spectacle. Did ever a tent, since the days of Cleopatra, contain such feminine charms? Was ever the circle of Old Drury studded with such brilliant gems? Those are no fictitious roses which compose that head-dress, and it is the livelier tinge of the un-rouged check which makes those roses blush. Let me direct your attention to that sweet girl opposite, just under the eaves of the pavilion, seven seats to the right of that ill-assorted patch. *Simplex munditiis*! How simple in her adornment! A single pale flower is in her jet-black hair, and her eyes were too dark, did not the softest lashes attemper their lustre. Alas! 'consumption, like a worm in the bud, feeds on her damask cheek!' And yet she knows it not. Light-hearted, she frequents the place of merriment, and mingles sportively in the dance. But she will pass away as doth a leaf, in autumn, or with the milder breath of spring. Her companions will lament her, and they will pluck the garland of the May-queen to pieces, to scatter it upon the grave.

These thoughts are sadly out of place, but grim death will be thrusting his visage every where, and there are goblins every masquerade. But there is nothing spectral in the looks of Helen——. She is seventeen, and very beautiful, and wild as a roe. Health sparkles in her eye, and riots in the rich bloom of her cheeks. She has more suitors than Penelope, but in two words her character may be told. She is a COQUETTE. We might sit gazing in that quarter for ever, for it is very hard to withdraw one's eyes from the fair. They are sure to come back again, the truants;

yet for the present, let us turn them to the rougher sex. Behold that man of gigantic stature, near the entrance of the tent. He lately emigrated from Connecticut, and stands seven feet two inches in his shoes. He wears a cerulean blue coat, buttoned up to his nose, and a tall, steeple-loafed hat. *Sic inure ad astra.* To see him entering the village, in this plight, driving a team of jack-asses before a square box of a wagon, and sitting bolt upright on a load of pumpkins, you would be apt to call him, in the dialect of his own people, 'an almighty lengthy creatur,' When he walks through the aisle of the church on Sunday, he overtops the tallest man in the congregation, by a whole head. He will be a conspicuous mark here. See if the clown does not take cognizance of him, before the play is done.

There stands a dandy, his legs apart, and forming. with the ground an isosceles triangle. He wears straps a yard long, his breeches being that much too short, and a very vulgar broach in his false bosom. His guard chain dangles in festoons about his vest, and a brass chain is terminated in a great ornament in the region of his knees. Mark his confused look. He thinks every body is gazing at him. 'How will you swop watches, onsight onseen?'

There is a jolly butcher, and there a farmer, of ruddy complexion and cheerful aspect, whip in hand, covered with dust, who has ridden hard, after mowing all day in the meadow, to bring his wife and daughters to the circus. He is not afraid to contribute of his substance to the wants of the needy, nor to the amusement of his family, of whom he is justly proud. Next to him sits an old man, holding a beautiful little boy, four years old, upon his knee, answering all his questions, quieting all his fears. Look at that idiot boy, grinning luridly upon the scene, with lolling tongue and watery mouth wide open, and white, unmeaning eyes. Look at that old man, with neck bent immoveably upon his breast, and so he has lived for many, many years—a pitiable object. There is another unfortunate, as thin as grim death, who is the victim of a tape-worm. He can yet laugh, and shake his lean sides. Thus wise men and fools arc mingled in this epitome of a world. Let us turn to a more promising specimen of human nature; that fat, gouty old gentleman, so comfortably provided for; wild Harry he was called, in his youth. He quivers like a jelly, and one peal of hearty laughter, which he appears

upon the verge of, will shake him into dissolution. He resembles that remarkable delineation of 'Tam O'Shanter,' struck from the rough free-stone into very life, by Thom, the self-taught artist. I hope the clown wont look at him at him. Have mercy, I pray thee, dear Mr. Harlequin.! Indulge your facetious personalities upon the lean ones, who have room enough to expand in, and who can afford to split their sides a-laughing. But cast none of your ill-timed fooleries in that quarter. I doubt if he will hold together as it is, but if you throw at him the joke direct, Wild Harry is a dead man!

Are there any in the whole area who will experience more genuine satisfaction, than the descendants of Ham? They are huddled together in one corner, dark, cloud-like, a distinct people. How will smiles and pleasantry be diffused over their features, like light bursting from the darkness! How will the whites of those eyes be uprolled in extacy, those even teeth glisten like ivory, and laughter break forth from the bottom of their souls, every laugh being worth a dollar! There, there!—listen to that shout! An unfortunate cur, who has strayed inside by accident, has got his toes severely trampled upon, and lamentably yelping, and running the gauntlet, is kicked out of doors. It is high time that the performances commenced. 'Music! music!' shout the crowd; and the orchestra without more ado plays a national air. Another piece is performed, and the tramping of horses is heard without.

Do you remember the feelings which possessed you, so charmingly described in one of the essays of Elia, when, a child, you were taken for the *first time* to the theatre; when the green curtain was drawn, and the tardy musicians crept one by one from some subterraneous place into the orchestra, and at last the overture was over, and the bell rang, and the risen foot-lights burst upon the scene of enchantment? Such feelings of intense anticipation pervade the rural audience. For now all things are ready, the passage is cleared, and silence reigns within the pavilion. The horses are coming! 'Heavens! look at that white-haired, cat-eyed boy, on the very edge of the ring! He will certainly be run over.'

Leave him alone, leave him alone. He will take care of himself, I warrant you. Nought is never in danger. Tramp, tramp, tramp! There they come. Observe the grand entrée, by four-and-twenty Arabian horses, while the rustic mother claps

her infant to her breast, scared by these terrible sports. At the first irruption of the cavalcade, the audience are bewildered with the general splendor of the scene. The horses, beautifully marked and caparisoned, are obedient to the slightest will of the rider, and yet by their proud looks and haughty bearing, seem conscious of their lineage; while the equestrians vie with each other in rich costume, and their plumes dropping softly over their painted faces, make them as bright as Lucifer, in the eyes of the crowd. They ride gracefully, displaying to advantage their elastic forms, swollen into full proportion by exercise and training. As soon as the audience is sufficiently recovered to particularize the different members of the troop, they are attracted by the grotesque behaviour of the clown, who has got upon his horse the wrong way, and sits preposterously facing the tail. In this manner he slips on and off, encouraged with immense laughter. Next the remarks go round, and every one praises to his neighbor the remarkable lightness and agility of a juvenile equestrian. He has not yet completed his eleventh summer, and not a horseman in the troop can vie with him in daring. The ladies who adorn the dress circle, regard him with smiles and approbation. *O! pulchrum puerum!* What a fair boy! How his ringlets flutter over his brow, in beautiful dishevelment, fanned by the wanton breeze. They could almost pluck him from his flying steed, and arrest his course with kisses. So light and agile is he, that he appears not human, but, as he flies round the ring with a daring rapidity, and his snow-white trowsers and gemmed vest mingle-their colors, and become indistinct, he seems like an apple-blossom floating on the air. But look! look! What the devil is that fellow at, disrobing himself? He has kicked himself out of his pantaloons, and thrown away his coat, his horse flying all the while. 'Angels and ministers of grace defend us!' he is plucking off his very—shirt! Nay, nay, do not be so alarmed, nor turn away your heads, ye fair ones, timidly blushing. Look again, and behold a metamorphosis more wonderful than any in Ovid; for lo! he pursues his swift career in the flowing robes of a woman! And now the pony is to perform a no less wonderful exploit, and leap through a balloon on fire. But why should I enumerate all the feats of this wild crew? What with riding, leaping, vaulting, and the most astonishing pirouettes, the first part of the diversions is enacted in a charming style. Who can say that he is not satisfied thus far, or has not got the worth of his money? Not that jolly butcher, not that farmer, not that sedentary schoolman, who has materially assisted his digestion by laughing. 'There is no medicine so good as the genuine ha! ha!'

To me, who am a genuine lover of human nature, and who sit curtained round in a stage-box, as it were, unnoticed by every one, and noticing every one, there is a chuckling delight in looking, not upon the actors of the scene, but on the motley crowd, and listening to such speeches as are naturally drawn from the occasion.

'I'll tell you *one* thing, and that aint *two*,' remarks a spectator to his neighbor, 'that the boy is wonderful, but if the clown is n't the old one, he is a nigh kin to him.'

'That's a fact.'

'He can twist himself wrong side out, he can.'

'Ay, ay, you 're right there, and he can tie himself into a bow knot.'

'These fellows,' says another, 'have n't got no bones into their bodies; they are made of Ingen rubber.'

'Bill,' remarks the ostler to his barefooted companion, usually yclept Villiam Viggins, a very bad boy, 'fine sort of life, eh, Bill? What say to try fortunes with 'em ? Jeffries, the head man, gin me a fair offer this mornin' to go along with him, and see a little of the world, what I've always had a great hankerin' for, and the great folks of the world, and a sight of things that I and you never dreamed of, and wont never dream of, if we stay here from now to never. I say, Bill, I've a mighty great notion of it, and should be glad of you for your company. You are prudenter than I be, by a good sight; contrariwise I am a better bruiser than you be, though I say it. We should pull together han'somely, and make our fortunes. It's a-high time, Bill, that we should 'stablish a ch'racter. But what takes my eye, these circus-actors live like gentlemen. The crack their jokes, they do, drink their wine, and live on the fat o' the land. Why can't we do the same, Bill? I can't see what 's to perwent it. There's no two ways about it, and if it is not all true, just what I tell you, then your name's not Villiam Viggins. And then it must be mighty agreeable to be dressed in such fine clothes, and to ride on such flashy horses, and to have nothin' to do but to be looked at, and to be laughed at, and to go a-larkin' and a travellin', and seein' all the world, and to be admired at by all the girls in the country. I say, Bill, the notion

takes you, you dog; I see it does. And now come let 's go out, and have a glass o' beer, and a long nine betwixt us, and talk the matter over a little, afore the entertainments begin ag'in.'

'In the country where I was fetched up,' said the son of Anak, 'no such doings as these is permitted. Two years ago, come next May, a company of circus-actors crossed over the Sound, and come to Bozrah. They sot themselves down, but did n't stay long, I guess, before they were attacked by the town-officers, and sent packing. They pulled up stakes, and took away their duds, and never come back, as I know on. For the people sot their faces like a flint agin 'em. Some few was for letting them act, but Deacon Giles opposed the motion, and carried his p'int, and on the Sabbath followin' stopped a load of hay on full drive through the town of Bozrah.'

In such conversation and exchange of sentiments, the interval 'between the acts' is wiled away. The second part of the diversions is a fescennine dialogue, made up of alternate strokes of rude raillery, interspersed with songs and merriment, affording as keen a relish as the best Attic salt.

'De gustibus non disputandum.'** Last of all, comes' BILLY BUTTON, OR THE HUNTED TAILOR.' I forget the plot of this piece, exactly, which is yearly enacted with much acceptation in every considerable village in the country. There are some very good points about it, that never come amiss to a rural audience, as when the perverse pony shakes off the cabbaging tailor from his back, not allowing him to mount, or, dangerously acting on the offensive, chases him around the ring. And now the entertainments are about to conclude, let us indulge a wish that the ladies who have been seated near the crevices in the awning, may not catch their death a-cold, and that no evil whatever may result from the occasion. The clown bounces into the arena with a bow; doffs his harlequin aspect, and assumes the serious air of an every-day man. 'Ladies and gentlemen, the entertainments of the evening are concluded. We thank you for your polite attendance.' In a twinkling the canvass is rent down over your heads, the lights are extinguished, and while the equestrians are already preparing to depart to the next village, the motley assemblage moves homeward through the dark night, yelping like savages.

*It rushes wherever a doorway is given.
**One must not dispute about tastes.

Walt Whitman review of Dan Rice's Circus in Brooklyn, originally published in the newspaper *Life Illustrated,* August 30, 1856. Text from *New York Dissected,* edited by Emory Holloway and Ralph Adimari (New York: R. R. Wilson, 1936): 193–96

THE CIRCUS

To witness the feats of the Ring is, to a very large proportion of our people, the only public amusement which breaks the monotony of the year. The Circus is a national institution. Though originating elsewhere, and in ages long previous to the beginning of History, it has here reached a perfection attained nowhere else. The American Circus is well known in South America, Europe, and Australia. In India, where many of the jokes and feats of the Circus originated, we believe an American circus company has performed. The Clown, we feel very sure, is of Oriental origin. Doubtless, some of the funny things which we saw Mr. Dan Rice do, in his tent at East Brooklyn last week, have amused young humanity for a hundred years. Nothing is so tenacious of life as a joke.

Yes—we spent an evening perched on one of the excruciatingly narrow boards of Mr. Rice's big tent, and we must avow that we were entertained exceedingly, and that we saw nothing and heard nothing calculated to do harm to any human being. Once or twice there was perhaps an approach to a *double entendre* on the part of the clown, which should have been avoided. It may have been unintentional, however. The manager of such an establishment, which amuses a million persons a year, should regard himself somewhat in the light of a public instructor. He should consider that seven tenths of his audiences are *boys*, upon all of whom his performances produce a thrilling effect, and who will be likely to catch a moral tone, as well as the ingenious tricks, of the Ring. As a general rule, the clown's joke and the master's grandiloquent speeches are extremely virtuous and intensely patriotic—which makes it all the more desirable that the faintest appearance of indecency should be absolutely forbidden. The presence of ladies (in thousands) has tended no doubt to the purification of the circus. If clergymen—in country places—would make a point of attending the performances occasionally, it would have an excellent effect upon the performers, upon the audience, and upon themselves.

To illustrate the moral tone of the Ring, we may mention that the clown, Mr. Dan Rice, made a remark to the following effect: "You mustn't strike a man behind his back, nor hit him when he's down. They do so in Congress, but that isn't the way with the Brooklyn boys." It was observable that this sentiment, though it was shared by every individual present [,] did not call forth any very great applause—so entirely *a matter of course* did it seem.

All clowns, we are informed, are of the fillibuster persuasion. Mr. Rice made no secret of his opinion that "Cuby will one day be ours." The continent—the whole continent—and all beside the continent—seemed to be his political creed, and the boys applauded the same. But there was no depth to the feeling. It is what is called a "gag." Gag, gentle and verdant reader, is something which comic men fall back upon when their resources for making legitimate fun are exhausted. Most allusions to the American flag are gag; such are always applauded. A compliment to lovely woman is gag; it never fails to bring down the tent. A moral maxim is gag; it is certain to be audibly approved. Patriotism and peanuts, virtuous feeling and "tickets—twenty-five cents" are inseparable. Mr. Thackeray remarks upon the severely moral characters of the heroes in the plays performed at the cheap theatres of London. Everywhere the heart of humanity yearns toward goodness and glories in the deeds that honor the race.

There is no use in decrying the circus. Even if it were the bad thing which some narrow good people think it is, it could not be put down. It is exactly suited to the place it fills. Residing in Brooklyn, near where Dan Rice pitched his mighty tent, we had an opportunity of observing the intense interest which it awakened, and the intense delight which the performances gave. A week before its arrival, the fences broke out with bills announcing the coming of the "Great Show." From that day young Brooklyn was agog. On the evening when we formed one of a compressed mass of human beings melting under the tent, there was not a foot of space vacant. Seven thousand persons were present. They were seated in great, ascending circles around the ring—a stilled whirlpool of human faces. The mere seating of this vast concourse was a moral lesson. The quiet, easy way in which the regulations were enforced, the ready acquiescence of nearly every one in those regulations, the summary but passionless ejectment of any boy or youth who refused to observe them, the care taken of the ladies, the perfect order that prevailed everywhere, the universal *right feeling* of the audience, the manly civility of the attendants, were all admirable to witness. No policement were necessary, though a few were present. All was effected by the three or four employees of the circus.

The performances, we have said above were unexceptionable. But they were more than that—they were of remarkable excellence. Dan Rice, as a clown, is not equal to his reputation; his jokes were not of extra quality, and he pronounces the English language in a "stupen-jew-ous" manner. But the sight of such beautiful and sagacious horses as he has, is worth the time it costs. His riders, too, and strong men, and jugglers, and dancers, are all perfect in their several ways, and afford a lively evidence of what *practice* will enable men to do. It can do no harm to boys to see a set of limbs display all their agility. It is a pity, we admit, that the education of any man should be confined to his legs. It is a pity, we assert, that the education of any man should be confined to his brain. But if we do not scruple to let children see men, and go to school to men who have no other than a brain development, let us not refuse occasionally to let them attend the evening school of these wonderfully leg-developed individuals. A circus performer is the other half of a college-professor. The perfect Man has more than the professor's brain and a good deal of the performer's legs.

If, therefore, this circus of Mr. Dan Rice's is a fair specimen of the circuses going about the country, we conclude that the circus is, to say the least, not a bad thing. It might be better. It ought to be most scrupulously decent. The slightest looking toward impropriety should be promptly hissed down. But upon the whole we are glad we went, glad there was a circus in Brooklyn to go to, and glad that the circus is an established institution of the country. Something very good may come of it, by-and-by.

Billboard, March 28, 1903

THE GREAT "OPENING" OF THE GREATEST SHOW ON EARTH

NEW YORK, MAY 19—The Barnum & Bailey Show signaled its return to America yesterday with characteristic éclat. It opened in a flashing blaze of brilliancy. Madison Square Garden was the scene of the ceremonies. In writing of the event, one understands why the circus press agent is habitually accused of grandiloquence. The function is so extraordinary; so entirely without parallel. The description coached in ordinary language fails utterly. Everyday words and phrases may suffice for everyday happenings, but when called upon to convey an idea of the grandeur, greatness, brilliancy, and especially the many-sided, ever-vary-lug[sic] and beautiful features of an entertainment so far beyond or out of the ordinary' the writer simply has to call upon words that have not had all the force ground out of them by constant usage. Anyone who charges the press agents of the Barnum & Bailey Shows with extravagance or bombast knows not their task—cannot conceive the difficulties under which they labor. They live in a world which is real and yet full of unrealities. They are surrounded by paradoxes. They breath an atmosphere charged with superlative. It is small wonder that their language and style betake somewhat of their environment. The real wonder is that the limitations of the dictionary and the hopeless inadequacy of words does not drive them to despair.

But to get back to the matter in hand, never was returning monarch more royally received by royal subjects. The big show re-entered the kingdom in truly regal style. A first-night audience, usually highly critical in New York, caught the spirit of the occasion and was unbounded in its demonstrations of approval. Each individual vied with his neighbor in voicing his vociferous approval. The vast auditorium resounded again and again with wild bursts of applause. The people were jubilant. They were please with everything. They applauded everything. Even the few "hitches" and waits unavoidable with a mammoth first production were not only charitably tolerated but actually approved.

It was a "Home Coming Celebration" and the audience considered itself as participant in the ovation. They were there to welcome the "big thing" in becoming style and they did it—not only once, but time and again. Wave after wave of applause passed over the auditorium and shook the vast and solid edifice to its foundations.

As the entertainment wore on the enthusiasm grew and widened. It became deafening, cyclonic in intensity. Men shouted themselves hoarse, youths stamped, whistled, and howled in paroxysms of delight and women waved handkerchiefs wildly. The scene cannot be described. It was at once a tribute and a triumph. It is safe to say that nothing like it has ever been seen.

The ceremonies were in every way as imposing as the event was auspicious.

The audience was made up of all classes from the newsboys and street gamins in the sky gallery, to the wealth and beauty of fashion in the boxes. The smart set were out in force. Style, elegance, handsome gowns, flashing jewels—all were in as great, if not greater evidence, than at a horse show or other exclusively fashionable function.

And the show! What gifted pen shall describe it? Where is the word painter that can portray its composite impression? Taken as a whole it cannot be pictured. To dissect and coldly catalogue it piece by piece seems almost sacrilege.

It opens with the spectacle designed and produced under the personal supervision of Mr. Bolossy Kiralfy.

It is entitled the Tribute of Balkis, and is aptly and justly termed in the program, "A glorious illuminated page from ancient history." It is gorgeous and magnificent to the last degree. It transcends and surpasses anything and everything that has ever been done along similar lines in the past. The costumes are superbly beautiful, the armor and chariots truly magnificent, the vast chorus of trained voices is equal to any in opera anywhere and the ballet is made up of the most finished product of the European dancing schools. Such a wealth of color, such a riot of plumes and feathers and armor is hard to imagine. The accessories alone must have cost several fortunes. Camels, dromedaries, elephants, sacred cattle, handsomely trapped horses in lavish profusion, all contributed to the picturesqueness of the scene. It is a fitting prelude to a prodigious program. Display number two fills the three rings with highly trained elephants in astonishing feats of posturing. Display number three is the leaps. "What!" you say, "An old time

leaping act?" Yes, just that but with this exception. EVERY LEAPER IS A DOUBLE SOMERSAULT LEAPER AS ARE ALSO TWO OF THE CLOWNS. The act is only allowed three minutes and "goes" like a house afire.

Display number four introduces three excellent lady riders to wit, Ella Bradna, Flora Bedini, and Bertha Clark. Their riding is excellent. This number also brings on the clowns. They are numerous and work well.

Display number five fills the rings, stage and hippodrome track with all sorts and kinds of acts, fourteen high-class acts going on at one and the same time, and all of them high-class. Here they are: Chas. Clark, juggler; Emma Sutcliffe, contortionist; The Dinus Troupe acrobats; Three Avolos, the horizontal bars; Shocki Japanese juggler; Three Marvelles, legomania; Avi, curious Japanese special performance; Leonard Bros., horizontal bars; Mons. Forrest, equilibrist; Percy Clark, hand balancer; Yokohama, barrell kicker; Young Friskey, umbrella juggler. The plethora of acts and actors in this display is remarkable. There are twenty-four straight performers and clowns galore. The abundance of the show—the bountiful plentitude is here exemplified and astonishes and bewilders.

Display number five introduces simultaneously five manege acts. The acts ridden by the Herzogs are very fine. Much new stuff is introduced and the horses surpass in training any thing that has ever been seen in America before. Josephine Koubeck is also entitled to special mention. While Rosa Hueltemann created a furore with the skipping rope horse "Baquette." Our own Madame Marantette the only American artist in the display, holds her own with the best of them. Her's is a driving meageact hippodrome track, and is highly interesting. Under her deft reins "Evergreen" a remarkable horse, shows eighteen different gaits. Between the displays Sam Watson gets a hand on his clowning with a goose.

Display number seven completely fills the dome of the garden with a great array of aerial acts. Those participating are Shocki, Seigrist-Silbon troupe, Alfred & John Sutcliffe Troupe, Arline Carroll, Herbert, Tonko and Little Leo.

Display number eight brings out the male riders, Fred Berrick, Wm. Wallett and Wilkes Lloyd. They are splendid riders.

Display number nine is given over to trained animal acts. Mons. Herzog works

a foot ball phony. Sam Watson introduces a cat that rides a dog. Miss Lloyd works a troupe of high-jumping wolf hounds, Ella Bradna displays some trained pigeons, and Sam Bennett works a pony.

Display number ten introduces Mons. Herzog and Helen Gerard, the latter in a driving manege. This is a beautiful act well rendered by a beautiful young woman and is a big bit. It is made more interesting by a number of dogs that work with it.

Display number eleven is an aerial number, given over to the Seigrist-Silbon Troupe, the Ryan-Zorella Troupe, and the Herbert Troupe. All are very good.

Display number twelve is devoted to three remarkably well ridden jockey acts, full of surprises and new stuff. Wilkes Lloyd is in ring number one, Wm. Wallett is in ring number three and the center ring is occupies by Mlle. Hogini and Victor Bedini. The property men, object holders and assistants are attired in English huntsmen's costumes which gives a gay coleratur to the scene and heightens its effect.

Display number thirteen is another big one. The Florence Troupe, Yokohama & Kiko, the Seven Sutcliffes, Uniski and Jess, the Three Marvels, The Three Avolos, The Leffee Trio and The Melnottes participate and Cyclo the kinetic demon winds it up. Cyclo's act is an elaboration of the cycle whirl and is an unparalleled exhibition of riding. It fairly carried the house off its feet.

Display number fourteen is given over to trained horses. Frank Melville's seventy horse act occupies the center and the Herzogs the two ends. The Herzog horses are remarkably handsome coal-black horses and they do many tricks new to America.

Display number fifteen is an aerial number. The Herbert Troupe and Ryan and Zorella are splendid, while the Clarkonians are astonishing to a degree. The performance of this duo of artists is truly marvelous and sensational. It was received with wild acclaim and applauded furiously.

Display number sixteen consists of exhibitions of ground acrobatic acts by three world-famous troupes. The Dinus Troupe of four men and two women, The Florenz Troupe of six men and one woman, and Grunatho Sisters, seven finely developed young women. All three troupes do most excellent work.

Display number seventeen is an exhibition of novel manege riding by Helen

Gerard and Mons. Herzog. Both display rare accomplishments. The acts conclude with a tableau finish of remarkable beauty.

Display number eighteen is a most tremendous aerial number. It is very heavy, very complicated and very ornate. In point of number of participants, it is doubtless the biggest aerial act ever exploited, but in spite of lots of real good stuff in it, it does not enthuse nor impress as one would think it should.

The Hippodrome concludes this most remarkable entertainment. Even this feature is freshened up with much stuff which if not new, is done in new ways—offered in new guise. The trappings are very handsome, the horses superb and speedy and the hippodrome as a whole full of fire and thrills. If one is inclined to protest against this somewhat hackneyed finish to an entertainment so novel and new in its entirety, he will find upon sitting it through that it is the idea that he resents and not the hippodrome itself.

Frank Melville is entitled to a very great credit for the way he handled the big mass of acts. He got the show in and out with remarkably few waits. Carl Clair's band also is deserving of great praise.

The remarkable array of clowns, jesters and buffoons is worthy in every way. Men of the very highest ability and gifts are found among them. Real talent is everywhere discernible. Among those that are especially good may be mentioned: Spader Johnson, Musical Clown; William Harvey, Bumpkin; Charles Harvey, Loon; Samuel Watson, August Clown; Forresto Innocente, French Comique; Frederick Martens, Funny Fred; Lizzie Seabert, Lady Clown; Chas. Wertz, Herlequin; Harry Friskey, Grimacer; Welda Dinus, Lady Clown; Sego Carlos, German Broad Face; Frank Leffel, Merry Andrew; Chas. Leffel, Austrian Looby; Albert Leffel, Funny Rustic; Charles Ryan, Odd Zany; Alexander Seabert, Fat Boy; F. W. Stelling, Pierrot; Rohelia Judge, Unique; Peter Bell, Children's Favorite; Robert Leo, Little Leo; Frank Oakley, Grimaldi; Billy Leonard, English Punch; Chas. Leonard, The Hot One; Art Adair, Motley Fool.

Most of the clowns are foreign artists hence it is particularly gratifying to be able to state that the American jesters in the bunch are the brightest of the bunch. Sammy Watson is a hit; Chas. Leonard is especially well received and Frank Oakley (Slivers) is the undoubted star of the contingent.

He does a snake charming act this season that would make a wooden man laugh.

THE MENAGERIE

The basement of the garden was to have been given over to the menagerie but was found to be inadequate. After crowding in the camels used in the spectacular, the 24 performing elephants, llamas, sacred cattle and two fine giraffes, it was found that there was only room left for the open dens (24 of them). Not a single cage could be exhibited. It is of course a great exhibit as it is, but not nearly so extensive as it will be on the road.

THE MUSEUM

The big chamber that was formerly given over to the bar and cloak room had to be pressed into service to accommodate the freaks and curious. Geo. Arlington presents a great array of them. He has gathered together the most complete line of novelties that has ever been seen in one exhibition. Evidence of the same lavish outlay discernible in the big show is found here. The same disregard of expense. The motto is "get the best and plenty of it." The fittings of the rooms alone represent a small fortune. There are electric lights of many colors, bunting palms and festooning. Brass rails and costly curtains and hangings help to set off the exhibits and the models of the U.S. war vessels serve the double purpose of ornaments and curious.

The actual program in this case gives a more accurate idea of the extensiveness of the museum than any amount of generalities. This list is actual. It is not padded in one single instance.

1. Imperial Russian Dancers. Eight Russian peasants in native garb who sing and dance.
2. Harvath Troupe of Midgets. Six diminutive specimens of humanity.
3. Hugo—French Giant. He is not only very tall but is broad and big.
4. Mohammed. Arab Dervish.
5. Chas. Tripp. Armless Wonder.
6. Zip. Original "what is it"
7. Tomasso. Human pincushion.
8. The Howards. Living Pictures.
9. Lionel. The Lion faced boy.
10. Loretta. Snake Charmer.
11. Korean Twins. Similar to the Siamese Twins.
12. Young Herman. The expansionest.
13. The Moss Haired Girl. Very odd.
14. Gardnier. Modern Samson.
15. John Hayes. Tatooed Man.
16. Eli Bowen. Legless wonder.
17. Mlle. Clifford. Human Ostrich.
18. Jas. Norris. Elastic skin man.
19. Grace Gilbert. Bearded Lady.
20. Wm. Doss. Human telescope.
21. Krao, the missing link.
22. Rob Roy. Albino dislocationist.
23. Beautiful Marie. Fat Woman.
24. Moxey. Needle eater.
25. Beatrice. Leopard girl.
26. Billy Wells. Anvil headed man.
27. Miraphone. A musical instrument made up of whirling wheels of different tones, played by a male and female artist.
28. Marconi, wireless telegraph station.
29. Ludger Sybaris, sole survior of the Mount Pelee disaster at Martinique.

A piano, two bag pipers, the Miraphone and other devices furnish music. It is a most wonderful exhibition.

Lack of space forbids a more extended account of this event. We could fill one entire issue of the paper and then not do the subject justice.

RETROSPECTIVE

In looking back at the entertainment after the lapse of three days, the impressions that are most lasting are the bigness and the bountifulness of it all. Never in the history of the business has there been such a 'whole lot,' such a 'great plenty' of show offered in an entertainment.

Where every act is a feature act it is of course hard to pick out acts of special excellence. But in spite of this, there are three that stick out of the mass and rank above all the others. They are the spectacle, Cyclo and the Clarkonians.

If all the rest of the show failed these features would yet save it.

Throughout the entire show, the touch of the master, James A. Bailey is everywhere seen. The boldness of it all is his. So too, it its balance and the nicety of its arrangement. Its wonderful abundance and its gorgeousness are due to his lavish expenditure. He is a wonderful man. With him at its helm, the Barnum & Bailey Show will always be a wonderful show.

Particularizing as The Billboard must needs to in giving its account in an opening always fails to do justice to the event as a whole. We present the foregoing with apologies. It is bare, bald and lifeless.

Brooks Atkinson review of the Ringling Bros. and Barnum & Bailey Circus, *New York Times*, April 19, 1942

GOING TO THE CIRCUS
Pandemonium and Elephants Prevail in The Modernized Ringling Show

WITHOUT the crowds the circus would lose character. For the crowds are quivering with excitement even in the streets outside Madison Square Garden. When we whirled up for an afternoon performance the taxicab could not find an empty space near the curb and proceeded to debouch us in the middle of the street. Before we could open the door an overwrought doorman and a passionate policeman rushed up to give us a good lacing. The excitement all around was infectious. The shrill clamor of hundreds of voices filled the capacious lobby, where grown people and children were weaving around in close-packed confusion. Every one seemed to be searching in vain for some one else, apprehensive of the worst. It was like arriving at a disaster where every one was unstrung.

Traffic Problems

Although the ticket wickets appeared to be hopelessly blocked, eventually it was possible to pass through into the magic land where the circus was on view. But the bedlam and confusion inside were worse. Traffic was heavy and competitive. The immediate problem was to get down to the basement where the animals and freaks were holding court. At the top of the stairs more people appeared to be coming up than were going down; but at the bottom of the stairs the proportions were reversed. This seemed contrary to nature, but it was true and alarming. Every one and his wife and children were on the loose, pushing, shouting, waving souvenir hats or canes, munching peanuts or plunging into cornucopias of spun sugar.

There wasn't space enough in the basement to speak a word of three syllables. But it was a relief to see the elephants. On one side of a long corridor they were gazing with friendly patience at the mob. Although the circus consists of many things, elephants are fundamental. No malevolent gorilla or savage lion, however spectacular, can represent the circus so confidently. The Ringlings are no fools. They give you elephants in a stupefying mass. You need never be famished for elephants under their house-flag.

The Elephants

And there they were—huge, gray, wrinkle-skinned, neatly barbered, gentle and kindly, obligingly taking peanuts from tiny hands. Do elephants like to be admired? If not, they might as well try. One elephant was lounging in silent melancholy against a concrete post, his eyes closed and his trunk resting limp on the floor. Like Poohbah, almost, he seemed to be thinking: "Go away, little people. Can't talk to little people like you." But the rest of the elephants who were restlessly moving on their great, padded feet, treated the crowd with impassive amiability. The little lady of three winters who headed our party fed them peanuts with dainty reverence. They seemed to be as much a part of her small world as the teddy-bear she takes to bed at night. It is the triumph of the circus elephant that little children do not fear him.

When the Ringlings announced two years ago that they were going to modernize the circus, many people, particularly if they had not been to the circus for a decade, took it as a personal affront. As it turns out, they were worrying about nothing. It was high time to modernize the circus, or to Americanize it, which amounts to the same thing. Norman Bel Geddes, the superman of Adrian, Mich., went to work on it last year, and John Murray Anderson, the peerless régisseur, is working at circus life for the first time this season. What they have given us is the handsomest and fleetest circus of—well, call it the ages. (This circus vernacular gets contagious.) It is drenched in blue sawdust, which gives it a feeling of restful splendor, and the pastel costumes are modern and beautiful. By varying the lighting Mr. Anderson has broken up the sheer mass of the spectacle and directed attention to the most breathtaking events.

Three-Year-Old Dismissed

He may be interested to know that the three-year-old critic carried as supercargo by this department was interested in the performance when all the lights were blazing, but when the lighting was concentrated in spots she squirmed, wriggled, banged the seat up and down and stuck her foot in the neck of the gentleman in front, thereby violating good neighbor policy. In about an hour her critical faculties were exhausted; for the good of the service she was relieved of further responsibility. It takes longer than you would think to train a durable critic.

Fundamentally Sound

But modernizing the circus has not changed the nature of the entertainment provided. Alfred Court's "implacable enemies of jungle wilds, educated beyond belief" (do those magnificent Great Danes come from the jungle?); the performing ponies and the scholarly sea lions; the death-defying aerialists and the bareback-riding wizards, garnished by troupes of clowns who are never as funny as you expect them to be—all this is good, fundamental circus. George Balanchine and Igor Stravinsky have collaborated on the "choreographic tour de force" of an elephant ballet by hanging some silly skirts on the noble beasts and writing some new dissonances for the brass band. But don't worry: it is still an act of performing elephants, and the skirts and the girls do not ruin it much. Take warning, Balanchine: elephants do not forget, and you cannot tell by the expression on their faces when they are ready to strike.

Too Much of Everything

Not that the details of a circus performance greatly matter. "Let's Face It" and "Best Foot Forward" are more exhilarating shows. But nothing save the circus can overpower you with such a tremendous mass of entertainment. It is the genius of the circus to give too much of everything. Take the excellent pageant of holidays, which Mr. Geddes has invented and costumed with princely prodigality— coaches so long that they can hardly get through the portals and turn, castellated floats with smiling blondes riding by, hundreds of walking mummers, a wagon of clangorous chimes, an honest calliope wreathed in live steam. Stupendous, that's the word for it! Meanwhile, the brass band is always blaring *fff*, the 'hawkers are bellowing and the audience is roaring with pleasure and astonishment. If an air raid occurred no one would notice it amid the normal bedlam. "Greatest show on earth" is no idle boast.

Acknowledgments

This exhibition and book would never have come to pass without contributions of many individuals and institutions. First and foremost, Susan Weber saw the promise of such an exhibition, and her enthusiasm, as well as her contributions to the content and interpretation, saw the project through from start to finish. The vibrant intellectual community that is the Bard Graduate Center made it a wonderful place to work. I would like to thank the faculty for their advice and support, namely Aaron Glass, Peter Miller, Andrew Morrall, Amy Ogata, Paul Stirton, and Ittai Weinryb. David Jaffee helpfully commented on an early draft of this catalogue and was my go-to source for questions about nineteenth-century New York and material culture. Elena Pinto Simon offered several leads and much encouragement. Tom Tredway and Karyn Hinkle facilitated a stream of book and interlibrary loan requests. Barb Elam and Terrance D'Ambrosio assisted with scanning and cataloguing materials, while Rick Barley and Gisela Schmidt provided timely technical support. Ken Ames was a source of support, good cheer, and sage advice throughout.

My greatest debt, though, is to the superlative staff in our exhibitions department. Nina Stritzler-Levine judiciously guided this project throughout, and I would have been at a loss without Olga Valle Tetowski's organizational expertise. I would also like to thank Ann Marguerite Tartsinis, Earl Martin, and Han Vu for their various contributions. Eric Edler ably handled all of the loans and Ian Sullivan designed a wonderful exhibition. Alexis Mucha collected all of the images, answered endless questions, and has been a great friend since I arrived at the Bard Graduate Center. I would also like to thank Laura Grey

for all of her hard work designing the catalogue and Barbara Burn for her sharp editing. Several students and research assistants helped on the project, and I would like to thank Andrew Goodhouse, Shoshana Greenwald, Sequioa Miller, Christie Wilmot, and Amber Winick, for their efforts.

Many others—curators, researchers, collectors, historians, and archivists—contributed to this project. I would like to thank Doug Clouse, Ralph Sessions, and Kristin Spangenberg for lending their expertise. Although the assorted institutions and many scholars who helped make this exhibition possible are listed below, I would like to thank a number of people in particular. At the American Antiquarian Society, Megan Bocian and Lauren B. Hewes facilitated access to and shared their knowledge about that institution's rich collection of early circus posters. Jennifer Lemak and John Scherer helpfully provided guidance at the New York State Museum. Amy Fulkerson helped to acquaint me with the Hertzberg Circus Collection held by the Witte Museum and was instrumental in securing objects for the exhibition. Micah Hoggatt was a great help in navigating the Harvard Theatre Collection, and Clayton Lewis of the Clements Library at the University of Michigan raised a timely concern about a performer jacket that made for a very interesting story. Peter Shrake at the Circus World Museum and Kory Rogers at the Shelburne Museum both provided able assistance in negotiating the circus collections at their respective institutions. At the John and Mable Ringling Museum of Art, Jennifer Lemmer-Posey and Deborah Walk helped uncover a wealth of material for the exhibition. Last but not least, I would like to thank Grace Zimmerman of the

Somers Historical Society for allowing me to explore that institution's wonderful collection of early American circus material and for facilitating a large number of loans for the exhibition.

The many members and friends of the Circus Historical Society provided invaluable assistance and advice. In particular, I would like to thank Chris Berry, David Carlyon, Bob Cline, Neil Cockerline, Stephen Flint, Judy Griffin, John Polascek, Richard Reynolds, Robert Sabia, William Slout, and Lane Talburt. Paul Ingrassia generously provided the magazine from which the photograph used as the frontispiece of this catalogue was taken. Fellow board member Fred D. Pfening III charitably loaned materials for the exhibition and shared his considerable knowledge of circus history.

Although he was not directly involved with this project, almost everything I know about nineteenth-century U.S. cultural history I learned from Jay Cook during my time at the University of Michigan. Brett Mizelle, Susan Nance, Gregory Renoff, and the other contributors to the companion volume all shaped my thinking about the larger history of the American circus. Through a combination of her scholarship and encouragement of my own, Janet Davis also shaped this catalogue in significant ways. My greatest thanks, however, are owed to Fred Dahlinger, whose broad knowledge of circus history was invaluable and who patiently answered a stream of inquiries and suggested countless objects and ideas that were incorporated into the exhibition.

Lastly, I would like to thank my friends and family. Although the circus is an endlessly fascinating topic to me, I am sure many of those around me over these last few years felt differently.

I am grateful to Dave Belding, Matt Ides, and Eric Rekeda for helping me through some stressful times. My sister, Kelly, her family, and my parents, Bill and Marilyn, were unflagging in their support. My greatest debt, however, is owed to Charlotte Trautman, whose combination of patience and assistance were invaluable in bringing this project to fruition. I hope that visitors to the exhibition and readers of this catalogue will enjoy the experience as much I have putting it together and that it will inspire further exploration of the colorful and compelling history of the circus in the United States.

The generous institutional and private lenders to the exhibition and the staff that facilitated the loans were; Albany Institute of History & Art: Tammis Groft, Nycole Kinns; American Antiquarian Society: Lauren B. Hewes, Jaclyn Penny; American Numismatic Society: Robert Hoge, Elena Stolyarik; AXA Equitable: Pari Stave; Barnum Museum: Melissa Houston, Kathleen Maher, Adrienne Saint-Pierre; Chris Berry; Big Apple Circus, Ltd.: Joel W. Dein, Philip Thurston; Brooklyn Museum: Elisa Flynn, Barry Harwood, Ruth Janson, Arnold L. Lehman; Brown University, John Hay Library: Rosemary Cullen, Rachel Lapkin; Circus World Museum: Steve Freese, Peter Shrake; Currier Museum of Art: Cindy Mackey, Karen Papineau, Andrew Spahr, Susan Strickler, Kurt J. Sundstrom; The Henry Ford: Leslie S. Mio, Jim Orr, Charles Sable, Kathy Steiner; International Center of Photography: Erin Barnett, Claartje van Dijk, Brian Wallis; Library of Congress: Rachel Waldron; Walter Zvonchenko; The Metropolitan Museum of Art: Thomas P. Campbell, Emily Foss, George R. Goldner, Constance McPhee, Freyda Spira, Mary Zuber; National Gallery of Art: Peter Huestis, Lisa M. MacDougall, Earl A. Powell III; National Portrait Gallery, Smithsonian Institution: Molly Grimsley, Lizanne Reger, Kristin L. Smith, Martin E. Sullivan; New-York Historical Society: Jean Ashton, Stephen R. Edidin, Eleanor Gillers, Susan Kriete, Heidi Nakashima, Marisa Schwartz, Scott Wixon; New York State Museum: Robyn Gibson, Jennifer Lemak, John Scherer; Fred D. Pfening III; Ringling Museum of Art: Françoise Hack, Steven High, Jennifer Lemmer-Posey, Heidi Taylor, Deborah W. Walk; Shelburne Museum: Thomas Denenberg, Jacquelyn Oak, Kory Rogers, Katherine Taylor-McBroom; Somers Historical Society: Meg Timone, Grace Zimmerman; Spencer Museum of Art: Janet K. Dreiling, Stephen H. Goddard, Saralyn Reece Hardy, Kate Meyer, Sherèe Peterson; The Strong: G. Rollie Adams, Richard R. Sherin, Lauren Sodano; Syracuse University Library: Nicolette A. Dobrowolski; Whitney Museum of American Art: Anita Duquette, Barbara Haskell, Matt Heffernan, Carol Mancusi-Ungaro, Adam D. Weinberg; William L. Clements Library, University of Michigan: J. Kevin Graffagnino, Clayton Lewis; The Witte Museum: Shellie Eagan, Amy Fulkerson; Yale Center for British Art: Timothy Goodhue, Amy Meyers.

Conservation work on objects and materials in the exhibition was performed by the Northeast Document Conservation Center and by Patsy Orlofsky of the Textile Conservation Workshop.

In terms of visual materials, Bruce White did a wonderful job photographing many of the objects pictured in the catalogue. Peter Angelo Simon granted permission to use a fine photograph from his series documenting the birth of the Big Apple Circus and Noel Daniel generously provided a photograph of Tiny Kline's "slide for life" over Times Square. For help with other images, I would like to thank the American Museum of Natural History: Alexa Metrick, Gregory Raml; Art Institute of Chicago: Jacqueline Maman; Brooklyn Public Library: Ivy Marvel; Hartman Center for Sales, Advertising & Marketing History, David M. Rubenstein Rare Book & Manuscript Library, Duke University: Liz Shesko; Houghton Library, Harvard University, Massachusetts: Susan Halpert, Micah Hoggatt; Milner Library, Illinois State University Special Collections: Maureen Brunsdale, Mark Schmitt; Missouri History Museum: Jaime Bourassa; Museum of the City of New York: Paul Mutino, Robbi Siegel; National Museum of American History, Archives Center, Smithsonian Institution: Kay Peterson; New York Public Library: Tom Lisanti, Stephan Saks; The New York Times/Redux: Rosemary Morrow; Princeton University Library, Rare Books and Special Collections: Charles Greene, Anna Lee Pauls; Tufts University Archives: Susane Belovari, Molly Bruce.

Bibliography

A Gentleman of Alfred, York County. *Murder of the Elephant: An Accurate Account of the Death of That Noble Animal, the Elephant*. Boston: Printed by Nathaniel Coverly, 1816.

Ablon, Joan. *Little People in America: The Social Dimension of Dwarfism*. New York: Praeger, 1984.

Adams, Bluford. *E Pluribus Barnum: The Great Showman and the Making of U.S. Popular Culture*. Minneapolis: University of Minnesota Press, 1997.

Adams, Philip R. *Walt Kuhn, Painter: His Life and Work*. Columbus: Ohio State University Press, 1978.

Albrecht, E. J. "Miles White: The Little Eccentric with the Big Talent." *Bandwagon* 37, no. 6 (November–December 1993), 50–60.

____. *The New American Circus*. Gainesville: University Press of Florida, 1995.

Allen, Robert C. "Motion Picture Exhibition in Manhattan 1906–1912: Beyond the Nickelodeon." *Cinema Journal* 18, no. 2 (Spring 1997), 2–15.

Amidon, Charles, and Stuart Thayer. "Early Parades, Early Bandwagons." *Bandwagon* 21, no. 6 (November–December 1977), 32–35.

"An Act to create a Fund in aid of the Society for the reformation of Juvenile Delinquents, in the City of New York and for other purposes." Passed April 29, 1829. *Laws of the State of New York Passed at the Fifty-First Session, Second Meeting, 1828 and Fifty-Second Session 1829*. Albany:

Printed by E. Croswell, Printer to the state for Wm. Gould & Co, 1829, 436–38.

Apps, Jerold W. *Ringlingville USA: The Stupendous Story of Seven Siblings and Their Stunning Circus Success*. Madison: Wisconsin Historical Society Press, 2005.

Ariano, Terry. "Beasts and Ballyhoo, The Menagerie Men of Somers." *Bandwagon*, 49, no. 1 (January–February 2005), 23–30.

Astley, Philip. *The modern riding-master: or, A key to the knowledge of the horse, and horsemanship; with several necessary rules for young horsemen*. Philadelphia: Robert Aitken, 1776.

Babinski, Tony. *Cirque Du Soleil: 20 Years Under the Sun*. New York: Harry N. Abrams, 2004.

Barker, Barbara. "Imre Kiralfy's Patriotic Spectacles: 'Columbus, and the Discovery of America' (1892–1893) and 'America' (1893)." *Dance Chronicle* 17, no. 2 (January 1, 1994), 149–78.

Barney, Brett. "Nineteenth-century Popular Culture." In *A Companion to Walt Whitman*, edited by Donald B. Kummings. Malden, MA: Blackwell Publishing, 2006.

Barnum's American Museum Illustrated. New York: n.p., 1850.

Barnum, P. T. *The Life of P. T. Barnum*. New York City: Redfield, 1855; repr. Buffalo: Courier, 1888.

____. *Struggles and Triumphs, or Forty Years' Recollections*. Buffalo, NY: Courier, 1875; repr. 1892.

____. *Selected Letters*. Edited by A. H. Saxon. New York: Columbia University Press, 1983.

Barratt, Carrie R., and Ellen G. Miles. *Gilbert Stuart*. New York: Metropolitan Museum of Art, 2004.

Barth, Miles. *Weegee's World*. Boston: Little, Brown, in association with the International Center of Photography, New York, 1997.

Beatty, Clyde, and Earl Wilson. *Jungle Performers*. New York: R. M. McBride, 1941.

Beckert, Sven. *The Monied Metropolis: New York City and the Consolidation of the American Bourgeoisie, 1850–1896*. Cambridge: Cambridge University Press, 2001.

Beecher, Henry W. *Lectures to Young Men: On Various Important Subjects*. Boston: J. P. Jewett, 1846.

Beers, Diane L. *For the Prevention of Cruelty: The History and Legacy of Animal Rights Activism in the United States*. Athens: Swallow Press, 2006.

Bender, Thomas. *The Unfinished City*. New York: New York University Press, 2007.

Benes, Peter, ed. *Itinerancy in New England and New York*. Boston: Boston University, 1986.

____. "To the Curious: Bird and Animal Exhibitions in New England, 1716–1825." In *New England's Creatures: 1400–1900*, edited by Peter Benes, 147–59. Boston: Boston University, 1995.

Berry, Chris. "Ringling Bros. and Barnum & Bel Geddes." *Bandwagon* 54, no. 6 (November–December 2011), 55–59.

A Biographical Sketch of I. A. Van Amburgh, and an Illustrated and Descriptive History of the Animals contained in the Menagerie…Now on Exhibition at Palace Gardens, 14th Street, N.Y. New York: Samuel Booth, 1862.

Block, Geoffrey. "'Bigger Than a Show—Better Than a Circus': The Broadway Musical, Radio, and Billy Rose's Jumbo." *Musical Quarterly* 89, nos. 2–3 (2006), 164–98.

Bogdan, Robert. *Freak Show: Presenting Human Oddities for Amusement and Profit.* Chicago: University of Chicago Press, 1988.

Braathen, Sverre O. *Here Comes the Circus!: The Rise and Fall of the Circus Band.* Evanston, IL: The Instrumentalist, 1958.

Bradley, Elizabeth L. *Knickerbocker: The Myth Behind New York.* New Brunswick, NJ: Rivergate Books, 2009.

Brown, T. Allston. *A History of the New York Stage.* New York: Benjamin Blom, 1903.

____. *Amphitheatres and Circuses: A History from Their Earliest Date to 1861, with Sketches of Some of the Principal Performers*, edited by William Slout. San Bernardino, CA: Borgo Press, 1994.

Bryan, J. III, "Sawdust Doll." *Collier's* (April 19, 1941), 13, 73–74.

Buckley, Peter G. "To the Opera House: Culture and Society in New York City, 1820–1860." PhD diss., State University of New York at Stonybrook, 1984.

____. "Paratheatricals and Popular Stage Entertainment." In *The Cambridge History of American Theatre*, edited by Don B. Wilmeth and C. W. E. Bigsby, 457. Cambridge: Cambridge University Press, 1998.

Bumgardner, Georgia Brady. "George and William Endicott, Commercial Lithography in New York 1831–1851." In *Prints and Printmakers of New York State, 1825–1940*, edited by David Tatham, 43–65. Syracuse, NY: Syracuse University Press, 1986.

Burrows, Edwin G., and Michael L. Wallace. *Gotham: A History of New York City to 1898.* New York: Oxford University Press, 1999.

Butsch, Richard. "Bowery B'hoys and Matinee Ladies: The Re-Gendering of Nineteenth-Century American Theater Audiences." *American Quarterly* 46, no. 3 (September 1994), 374–405.

____. *The Making of American Audiences: From Stage to Television, 1750–1990.* Cambridge: Cambridge University Press, 2000.

Cannato, Vincent J. *American Passage: The History of Ellis Island.* New York: Harper, 2009.

Carlyon, David. *Dan Rice: The Most Famous Man You've Never Heard of.* New York: Public Affairs, 2001.

Chemers, Michael M. "Jumpin' Tom Thumb: Charles Stratton Onstage at the American Museum." *Nineteenth Century Theatre and Film* 31, no. 2 (2004), 16–27.

____. *Staging Stigma: A Critical Examination of the American Freak Show.* New York: Palgrave Macmillan, 2008.

Clair, Jean, ed. *The Great Parade: Portrait of the Artist as Clown.* New Haven: Yale University Press, 2004.

Clarke, Norman. *The Mighty Hippodrome.* Cranbury, NJ: A. S. Barnes, 1968.

Conover, Richard E. *The Telescoping Tableaus: An Historical Note on the Big Circus Parade Wagons of the 1870's.* Xenia, OH: Conover, 1956.

____. *The Affairs of James A. Bailey.* Xenia, OH: Conover, 1957.

____. *The Fielding Bandchariots.* Xenia, OH: Conover, 1969.

Cook, James W. *The Arts of Deception: Playing with Fraud in the Age of Barnum.* Cambridge, MA: Harvard University Press, 2001.

____. "Dancing across the Color Line." *Common-Place* 4, no. 1 (2003), http://www.common-place.org/vol-04/no-01/cook/

Cook, James W., ed. *The Colossal P. T. Barnum Reader: Nothing Else Like It in the Universe.* Urbana: University of Illinois Press, 2005.

Cosdon, Mark. *The Hanlon Brothers: From Daredevil Acrobatics to Spectacle Pantomime, 1833–1931.* Carbondale: Southern Illinois University Press, 2009.

Coup, W. C. *Sawdust & Spangles: Stories & Secrets of the Circus.* Chicago: H. S. Stone, 1901.

Cowell, Joe. *Thirty Years Passed Among the Players in England and America.* New York: Harper & Brothers, 1844.

Crawford, Richard. *America's Musical Life.* New York: W. W. Norton, 2005.

Culhane, John. *The American Circus: An Illustrated History.* New York: Henry Holt, 1991.

Dahlinger Jr., Fred. "Short History of Steam Calliope History Before 1900." *Bandwagon* 16, no. 6 (November–December 1972), 25–27.

____. "The Development of the Railroad Circus, Part I." *Bandwagon* 27, no. 6 (November–December 1983), 6–11.

____. "The Development of the Railroad Circus, Part II." *Bandwagon* 28, no. 1 (January–February 1984), 16–27.

____. "The History of the Golden Age of Chivalry." *Bandwagon* 41, no. 2 (March–April 1997), 24–31.

Dahlinger Jr., Fred, and Richard Conover. "Pictorial Encyclopedia of Circus Parade Wagons." *Bandwagon* 13, no. 6 (November–December 1969), 14–17.

Dahlinger Jr., Fred, and Stuart Thayer. *Badger State Showmen: A History of Wisconsin's Circus Heritage.* Madison, WI: Grote Pub, 1998.

Davis, Elliot Bostwick. "The Currency of Culture: Prints in New York City." In *Art and the Empire City: New York, 1825–1861*, edited by Catherine H. Voorsanger and John K. Howat, 189–225. Exhibition catalogue. New York: Metropolitan Museum of Art, 2000.

Davis, Janet M. "Bearded Ladies, Dainty Amazons, Hindoo Fakirs, and Lady

Savages: Circus Representations of Gender and Race in Victorian American." In Spangenberg and Walk, *The Amazing American Circus Poster*, 75–84.

____. *The Circus Age: Culture and Society under the American Big Top*. Chapel Hill: University of North Carolina Press, 2003.

Davis, Janet M. ed. *Circus Queen & Tinker Bell: The Memoir of Tiny Kline*. Urbana: University of Illinois Press, 2008.

Davis, Susan G. *Parades and Power: Street Theatre in Nineteenth-Century Philadelphia*. Philadelphia: Temple University Press, 1986.

Day, Charles H. "Making Much of Music." *Billboard*, May 11, 1901.

Decastro, Jacob. *The Memoirs of J. Decastro, Comedian*. Edited by R. Humphreys. London: Sherwood, Jones, 1824.

DeMarlo, Friede. "Farewell to Glitter, Sawdust, and the World." Unpublished memoir. Popular Entertainment Collection, New York State Museum, Albany, NY.

Dennett, Andrea Stulman. *Weird & Wonderful: The Dime Museum in America*. New York: New York University Press, 1997.

Donald, Diana. *Picturing Animals in Britain, 1750–1850*. New Haven: Yale University Press for The Paul Mellon Centre for Studies in British Art, 2007.

Downer, Alan Seymour, ed. *The Memoir of John Durang, American Actor, 1785–1816*. Pittsburgh: University of Pittsburgh Press, 1966.

Du Bois, W. E. B. "The Problem of Amusement" (1897). Reprinted in *Du Bois on Religion*, edited by Phil Zuckerman, 19–25. Walnut Creek, CA: Alta Mira Press, 2000.

Dudden, Faye E. *Women in the American Theatre: Actresses and Audiences, 1790–1870*. New Haven: Yale University Press, 1994.

Duffy, Stephen. "Landseer and the Lion-Tamer: The 'Portrait of Mr. Van Amburgh' at Yale." *British Art Journal* 3, no. 3 (2002), 25–35.

Dunlap, William. *A History of the American Theatre*. New York: J. & J. Harper, 1832.

Durang, Charles. *Theatrical Rambles of Mr. & Mrs. Greene*, edited by William L. Slout. San Bernardino, CA: Borgo Press, 1987.

Durso, Joseph. *Madison Square Garden, 100 Years of History*. New York: Simon and Schuster, 1979.

Ernst, Robert. *Immigrant Life in New York City, 1825–1863*. Port Washington, NY: I. J. Friedman, 1965.

Estee, Charles F., ed. *The Excise Tax Law*. New York: Fitch, Estee, 1863.

Evans, Dorinda. *The Genius of Gilbert Stuart*. Princeton: Princeton University Press, 1999.

Fauquet, John-Stuart. "Elephants on Relief?: Circus and the WPA (1935–1939)." MA thesis, University of Wisconsin, 2007.

Flint, Richard W. "Entrepreneurial and Cultural Aspects of the Early-Nineteenth-Century Circus and Menagerie Business." In *Itinerancy in New England and New York*, edited by Peter Benes and Jane Montague, 131–49. Boston: Boston University Press, 1986.

____. "American Showmen and European Dealers: Commerce in Wild Animals in Nineteenth Century America." In *New World, New Animals: From Menagerie to Zoological Park in the Nineteenth Century*, edited by Robert J. Hoage and William A. Deiss, 97–108. Baltimore: Johns Hopkins University Press, 1996.

____. "A Great Industrial Art: Circus Posters, Business Risks, and the Origins of Color Letterpress Printing in America." *Printing History* 26 (2009), 18–43.

____. "Promoting Peerless Prodigies 'To the Curious.'" In Spangenberg and Walk, *The Amazing American Circus Poster*, 49–54.

Fox, Charles Philip, and Tom Parkinson. *Billers, Banners, and Bombast: The Story of Circus Advertising*. Boulder, CO: Pruett, 1985.

Fox, Richard Wightman. "The Discipline of Amusement." In *Inventing Times Square: Commerce and Culture at the Crossroads of the World*, edited by William R. Taylor, 83–98. New York: Russell Sage Foundation, 1991.

Fried, Frederick. *Artists in Wood: American Carvers of Cigar-Store Indians, Show Figures, and Circus Wagons*. New York: Clarkson N. Potter, 1970.

Frost, Hyatt. *A Biographical Sketch of I. A. Van Amburgh*. New York: Samuel Booth, 1862.

Gerber, David A. "The 'Careers' of People Exhibited in Freak Shows: The Problem of Volition and Valorization." In *Freakery: Cultural Spectacles of the Extraordinary Body*, edited by Rosemarie Garland Thompson, 38–54. New York: New York University Press, 1996.

Gilje, Paul A. *The Road to Mobocracy: Popular Disorder in New York City, 1763–1834*. Chapel Hill: University of North Carolina Press, 1987.

Glenn, Susan A. *Female Spectacle: The Theatrical Roots of Modern Feminism*. Cambridge, MA: Harvard University Press, 2000.

Gossard, Steve. *A Reckless Era of Aerial Performance: The Evolution of Trapeze*. Normal, IL: Steve Gossard, 1994.

Greenwood, Isaac J. *The Circus: Its Origin and Growth Prior to 1835*. New York: The Dunlap Society, 1898.

Gustafson, Donna, ed. *Images from the World between: The Circus in 20th Century American Art*. Cambridge, MA: MIT Press, 2001.

Haberly, Loyd. "The American Museum from Baker to Barnum." *New York Historical Society Quarterly* 43, no. 3 (July 1959), 24–30.

Hammarstrom, David L. *Big Top Boss: John Ringling North and the Circus*. Urbana: University of Illinois Press, 1992.

____. *Fall of the Big Top: The Vanishing American Circus*. Jefferson, NC: McFarland, 2008.

____. *Inside the Changing Circus: A Critic's Guide*. Duncan, OK: BearManor Media, 2012.

Harding, Les. *Elephant Story: Jumbo and P. T. Barnum Under the Big Top.* Jefferson, NC: McFarland, 2000.

Harris, Neil. *Humbug: the Art of P. T. Barnum.* Boston: Little, Brown, 1973.

Haskell, Barbara. *Milton Avery.* New York: Whitney Museum of American Art, in association with Harper & Row, 1982.

Haswell, Chas. H. *Reminiscences of New York by an Octogenarian, 1816 to 1860.* New York: Harper, 1896.

Hayner, Rutherford. *Troy and Rensselaer County, New York: A History.* 3 volumes. New York: Lewis Historical Pub., 1925.

Hazen, Margaret H., and Robert M. Hazen. *The Music Men: An Illustrated History of Brass Bands in America, 1800–1920.* Washington, DC: Smithsonian Institution Press, 1987.

Hearn, Michael P. *McLoughlin Brothers, Publishers, 1828–1978.* Los Angeles: Dawson's Book Shop, 1980.

Henderson, Mary C. *The City and the Theatre: New York Playhouses from Bowling Green to Times Square.* New York: Preston, 1982.

Henkin, David M. *City Reading: Written Words and Public Spaces in Antebellum New York.* New York: Columbia University Press, 1998.

Hill, Errol, and James V. Hatch. *A History of African American Theatre.* Cambridge: Cambridge University Press, 2003.

Hirschfeld, Charles. "America on Exhibition: The New York Crystal Palace." *American Quarterly* 9, no. 2 (1957), 101–16.

Hofer, Margaret K. *The Games We Played: The Golden Age of Board & Table Games.* New York: Princeton Architectural Press, 2003.

Hone, Philip. *The Diary of Philip Hone, 1828–1851.* Volume 2, edited by Allan Nevins. New York: Dodd, Mead, 1927.

Jando, Dominique. *Big Apple Circus— 25 Years.* New York: Big Apple Circus, in association with Odyssey Guides, 2003.

Jenkins, Reese. *Images and Enterprise: Technology and the American Photo-graphic Industry, 1839 to 1925.* Baltimore: Johns Hopkins University Press, 1975.

Jenkins, Stephen. *The Greatest Street in the World: The Story of Broadway, Old and New, from the Bowling Green to Albany.* New York: G. P. Putnam's Sons, 1911.

Jensen, Dean, and Rosalie Goldstein. *Center Ring, the Artist: Two Centuries of Circus Art.* Milwaukee: Milwaukee Art Museum, 1981.

Joys, Joanne. *The Wild Animal Trainer in America.* Boulder, CO: Pruett, 1983.

Kammen, Michael G. *American Culture, American Tastes: Social Change and the 20th Century.* New York: Alfred A. Knopf, 1999.

Kasson, John F. *Amusing the Million: Coney Island at the Turn of the Century.* New York: Hill & Wang, 1978.

Kattenberg, Burns M. "Forgotten Acrobats of the Arena." *Muscle Power* 8, no. 3 (Summer 1963), 18–19, 42–43.

Kelly, Emmett, with F. Beverly Kelley. *Clown.* New York: Prentice Hall, 1954.

Kelly, Rob Roy. *American Wood Type, 1828–1900: Notes on the Evolution of Decorated and Large Types and Comments on Related Trades of the Period.* New York: Van Nostrand Reinhold, 1969.

Kelty, Edward J., Miles Barth, Alan M. Siegel, and Edward Hoagland. *Step Right This Way: The Photographs of Edward J. Kelty.* New York: Barnes & Noble Books, 2002.

Kitchen, Robert. "19th Century Circus Bands and Music." *Bandwagon* 29, no. 5 (September–October 1985), 14–17.

Klamkin, Marian. *The Return of Lafayette, 1824–1825.* New York: Scribner, 1975.

Kotar, S. L., and J. E. Gessler. *The Rise of the American Circus, 1716–1899.* Jefferson, NC: McFarland, 2011.

Kunhardt Jr., Philip B., Philip B. Kunhardt III, and Peter W. Kunhardt. *P. T. Barnum: America's Greatest Showman.* New York: Alfred A. Knopf, 1995.

Kunzog, John C. *The One Horse Show.* New York: John Kunzog, 1962.

Lambert, John. *Travels through Canada, and the United States of North America, in the Years 1806, 1807, & 1808: To Which Are Added Biographical Notices and Anecdotes of Some of the Leading Characters in the United States.* 2 volumes. London: Printed for C. Cradock and W. Joy, 1814.

Last, Jay T. *The Color Explosion: Nineteenth-century American Lithography.* Santa Ana, CA: Hillcrest Press, 2005.

Leach, William. *Land of Desire: Merchants, Power, and the Rise of a New American Culture.* New York: Pantheon, 1993.

Lee, Anthony W., and Richard Meyer. *Weegee and Naked City.* Berkeley: University of California Press, 2008,

Lemak, Jennifer. "The Frog Lady and the Devil." *New York Archives* 11, no. 2 (Fall 2011), 10–13.

Lennie, Campbell. *Landseer: The Victorian Paragon.* London: Hamish Hamilton, 1976.

Levine, Lawrence W. *Highbrow/lowbrow: The Emergence of Cultural Hierarchy in America.* Cambridge, MA: Harvard University Press, 1988.

Lhamon, W. T. *Raising Cain: Blackface Performance from Jim Crow to Hip Hop.* Cambridge, MA: Harvard University Press, 1998.

____. *Jim Crow, American.* Cambridge, MA: Belknap, 2009.

Lindfors, Bernth, ed. *Africans on Stage: Studies in Ethnological Show Business.* Bloomington: Indiana University Press, 1999.

Lipman, Jean, and Nancy Foote. *Calder's Circus.* New York: E. P. Dutton, 1972.

Lipman, Jean, Elizabeth V. Warren, and Robert C. Bishop. *Young America: A Folk-Art History.* New York: Hudson Hills Press, in association with the Museum of American Folk Art, 1986.

Lott, Eric. *Love and Theft: Blackface Minstrelsy and the American Working Class.* New York: Oxford University Press, 1993.

Magri, M. Lavinia. *The Autobiography of Mrs. Tom Thumb*, edited and published by A. H. Saxon. Hamden, CT: Archon Books, 1979.

Marter, Joan M. *Alexander Calder*. Cambridge: Cambridge University Press, 1991.

Marzio, Peter C. *The Democratic Art: Pictures for a 19th-Century America: Chromolithography, 1840–1900*. Boston: David R. Godine, 1979.

May, Lary. *Screening Out the Past: The Birth of Mass Culture and the Motion Picture Industry*. New York: Oxford University Press, 1980.

McAllister, Marvin E. *White People Do Not Know How to Behave at Entertainments Designed for Ladies & Gentlemen of Colour: William Brown's African & American Theater*. Chapel Hill: University of North Carolina Press, 2003.

McCabe, James D. *Lights and Shadows of New York Life: Or, the Sights and Sensations of the Great City*. Philadelphia: National Pub. Co., 1872.

McConachie, Bruce A. *Melodramatic Formations: American Theatre and Society, 1820–1870*. Iowa City: University of Iowa Press, 1992.

McCullough, Jack W. *Living Pictures on the New York Stage*. Ann Arbor: UMI Research Press, 1983.

McKay, George L. *A Register of Artists, Engravers, Booksellers, Bookbinders, Printers & Publishers in New York City, 1633–1820*. New York: New York Public Library, 1942.

McKusick, Victor A., and David L. Rimoin. "General Tom Thumb and Other Midgets." *Scientific American* (July 1967), 103–10.

McVickar, H. W., and W. Launder. *Our Amateur Circus; or a New York Season*. New York: Harper & Brothers, 1892.

Miles, Ellen G., Patricia Burda, Cynthia J. Mills, and Leslie K. Reinhardt. *American Paintings of the Eighteenth Century*. Washington, DC: National Gallery of Art, 1995.

Mitchell, Michael. *Monsters: Human Freaks in America's Gilded Age: The Photographs of Chas Eisenmann*.

Toronto: ECW Press, 1979; repr. 2002.

Mizelle, Brett. "'I Have Brought my Pig to a Fine Market': Animals, Their Exhibitors, and Market Culture in the Early Republic." In *Cultural Change and the Market Revolution in America, 1789–1860*, edited by Scott Martin, 181–216. Lanham, MD: Rowman and Littlefield, 2004.

Monsos, Holly. "Miles White." In *Late & Great: American Designers 1960–2010*, edited by Bobbi Owen, 220–29. Syracuse, NY: U.S. Institute for Theatre Technology, 2010.

Moody, Richard. *The Astor Place Riot*. Bloomington: Indiana University Press, 1958.

Moreau, Charles C. *A Collection of Playbills & c., relating to the Circus in New York City*. New York, 1894.

Morris, Ron. *Wallenda: A Biography of Karl Wallenda*. Chatham, NY: Sagarin Press, 1976.

Moy, James S. "John B. Ricketts' Circus, 1793–1800." PhD dissertation, University of Illinois at Urbana-Champaign, 1977.

____. "Entertainments at John B. Ricketts's Circus, 1793–1800." *Educational Theater Journal* 30, no. 2 (May 1978), 186–202.

Nance, Susan. *How the Arabian Nights Inspired the American Dream, 1790–1935*. Chapel Hill: University of North Carolina Press, 2009.

"New Shine for the Circus." *Life* (June 20, 1955), 79–84.

The New York Society for the Prevention of Cruelty to Children, Incorporated by the Legislature. Third Annual Report, for the Year Ending December 31, 1877. New York: Styles & Cash, 1878.

North, Henry R., and Alden Hatch. *The Circus Kings: Our Ringling Family Story*. Garden City, NY: Doubleday, 1960.

Nowatzki, Robert. "Paddy Jumps Jim Crow: Irish-Americans and Blackface Minstrelsy." *Eire-Ireland* 41, nos. 3–4 (Winter 2006), 162–85.

Odell, George C. *Annals of the New York Stage*, 15 volumes. New York: Columbia University Press, 1927–49.

O'Nan, Stewart. *The Circus Fire: A True Story*. New York: Doubleday, 2000.

Osgood, Samuel. *New York in the Nineteenth Century*. New York: New-York Historical Society, 1867.

Parkinson, Greg. "A Legend is Born." *Bandwagon* 22, no. 3 (May–June 1978), 15–21.

Pecktal, Lynn. *Costume Design: Techniques of Modern Masters*. New York: Back Stage Books, 1993.

Peiss, Kathy L. *Cheap Amusements: Working Women and Leisure in Turn-of-the-Century New York*. Philadelphia: Temple University Press, 1986.

Pennsylvania Magazine of History and Biography 39, no. 4 (October 1915), 427.

Peters, Harry T. *America on Stone*. Garden City, NY: Doubleday Doran, 1931.

Pfening Jr., Fred D. "Circus Loop the Loop Acts." *Bandwagon* 13, no. 3 (May–June 1969), 20–24.

____. "Human Cannonballs, Part One." *Bandwagon* 20, no. 6 (November–December 1976), 4–15.

____. "The Famous Zacchinis." *Bandwagon* 22, no. 6 (November–December 1978), 4–14.

____. "Manhattan's Summer Circus Battle." *Bandwagon* 38, no. 2 (March–April 1994), 14–21.

Pfening III, Fred D. "The American Circus and the Great Depression: 1929–1939." MA thesis. Ohio State University, 1976.

____. "Our Covers." *Bandwagon* 54, no. 4 (July–August 2010), 2.

____. "The Strobridge Lithographing Company, The Ringling Brothers, and Their Circuses." In Spangenberg and Walk, *The Amazing American Circus Poster*, 36–37.

Phelps Stokes, I. N. *The Iconography of Manhattan Island, 1498–1909*. 6 volumes. New York: Robert H. Dodd, 1915–28.

Plowden, Gene. *Merle Evans: Maestro of the Circus*. Miami: E. A. Seemann, 1971.

____. *Circus Press Agent: The Life and Times of Roland Butler*. Caldwell, ID: Caxton Printers, 1984.

Poignant, Roslyn. *Professional Savages: Captive Lives and Western Spectacle*. New Haven: Yale University Press, 2004.

Presbrey, Frank. *The History and Development of Advertising*. Garden City, NY: Doubleday, 1929.

Reilly, Bernard. *Currier & Ives: A Catalogue Raisonné*. Detroit: Gale Research, 1984.

Renoff, Gregory J. *The Big Tent: The Traveling Circus in Georgia, 1820–1930*. Athens, University of Georgia Press, 2008.

Rosenheim, Jeff L. "'A Palace in the Sun': Early Photography in New York City." In *Art and the Empire City: New York, 1825–1861*, edited by Catherine H. Voorsanger and John K. Howat. 227–57. Exhibition catalogue. New York: Metropolitan Museum of Art, 2000.

Rulau, Russell. *Standard Catalog of United States Tokens, 1700–1900*. Iola, WI: Krause Publications, 1994.

Sanger, George. *Seventy Years a Showman: My Life and Adventures in Camp and Caravan the World Over*. London: C. Arthur Pearson, 1908.

Saxe, Stephen O., et al. *Billheads & Broadsides: Job Printing in the 19th-century Seaport*. exh. cat. New York: South Street Seaport Museum, 1985.

Saxon, A. H. *Enter Foot and Horse: A History of Hippodrama in England and France*. New Haven: Yale University Press, 1968.

____. "A Franconi in America: The New York Hippodrome of 1853." *Bandwagon* 19, no. 5 (September–October 1975), 13–17.

____. *The Life and Art of Andrew Ducrow & the Romantic Age of the English Circus*. Hamden, CT: Archon Books, 1978.

____. *P. T. Barnum: The Legend and the Man*. New York: Columbia University Press, 1989.

Saxton, Alexander. *The Rise and Fall of the White Republic: Class Politics and Mass Culture in Nineteenth-Century America*. London: Verso, 1990.

Scharf, J. Thomas, and Thompson Westcott. *History of Philadelphia, 1609–1884*. Volume 2. Philadelphia: L. H. Everts, 1884.

Scheiner, Seth M. *Negro Mecca: A History of the Negro in New York City, 1865–1920*. New York: New York University Press, 1965.

Scudder, John. *A Companion to the American Museum: Open for Public Inspection in the New-York Institution, Park, Broadway*. New York: G. F. Hopkins, 1823.

Sessions, Ralph. *The Shipcarvers' Art: Figureheads and Cigar-Store Indians in Nineteenth-Century America*. Princeton: Princeton University Press, 2005.

Shoshani, Sandra Lash, Jheskel Shoshani, and Fred Dahlinger Jr. "Jumbo: Origin of the Word, and History of the Elephant." *Elephant* 2, no. 2 (Fall 1986), 86–122.

Sights and Wonders in New York: Including a Description of the Mysteries, Miracles, Marvels, Phenomena, Curiosities, and Nondescripts, Contained in That Great Congress of Wonders, Barnum's Museum. New York: J. S. Redfield, 1849.

Simon, Peter Angelo. *Big Apple Circus*. New York: Penguin Books, 1978.

Slout, William L. *Clowns and Cannons: The American Circus during the Civil War*. San Bernardino, CA: Borgo Press, 1997.

____. *Olympians of the Sawdust Circle: A Biographical Dictionary of the Nineteenth Century American Circus*. San Bernardino, CA: Borgo Press, 1998.

____. *A Royal Coupling: The Historic Marriage of Barnum and Bailey*. San Bernardino, CA: An Emeritus Enterprise, 2000.

Snyder, Robert W. *The Voice of the City: Vaudeville and Popular Culture in New York*. New York: Oxford University Press, 1989.

Sobel, Bernard. *A Pictorial History of Burlesque*. New York: Bonanza Books, 1956.

Spangenberg, Kristin L., and Deborah Walk, eds. *The Amazing American Circus Poster: The Strobridge Lithographing Company*. Cincinnati: Cincinnati Art Museum, 2011.

Speaight, George. "The Origin of the Circus Parade Wagon." *Bandwagon* 21, no. 6 (November–December 1977), 37–39.

____. *A History of the Circus*. London: Tantivy Press, and San Diego: A. S. Barnes, 1980.

____. *The Book of Clowns*. London: Sidgwick and Jackson, 1985.

St. Leon, Mark. *Circus in Australia: May Wirth, the Bareback Queen*. Penhurst, NSW: Mark St. Leon, 2008.

Stansell, Christine. *City of Women: Sex and Class in New York, 1789–1860*. New York: Alfred A. Knopf, 1986.

Steen, Ivan D. "America's First World's Fair: The Exhibition of the Industry of All Nations at New York's Crystal Palace, 1853–1854." *New-York Historical Society Quarterly* 47, no. 3 (1963), 257–87.

Stewart, A. B., comp. *Diary or Route Book of P. T. Barnum's Greatest Show on Earth and The Great London Circus for the Season of 1882*, n.d., s.n.

Stott, Richard B. *Workers in the Metropolis: Class, Ethnicity, and Youth in Antebellum New York City*. Ithaca: Cornell University Press, 1990.

Studwell, William E., Charles P. Conrad, and Bruce R. Schueneman, eds. *Circus Songs: An Annotated Anthology*. New York: Haworth Press, 1999.

Sturtevant, C. G. "Elephants of the Circus." *White Tops* (1931), 6–10.

Swortzell, Lowell. *Here Come the Clowns: A Cavalcade of Comedy from Antiquity to the Present*. New York: Viking, 1978.

Tchen, John Kuo Wei. *New York Before Chinatown: Orientalism and the Shaping of American Culture, 1776–1882*. Baltimore: Johns Hopkins University Press, 1999.

Thayer, Stuart. "Some Class Distinctions in the Early Circus Audience." *Bandwagon* 23, no. 4 (July–August 1980), 20–21.

____. "'The Keeper Will Enter The Cage': Early American Wild Animal Trainers." *Bandwagon* 26, no. 6 (November–December 1982), 38–40.

____. "The Elephant in America Before 1840," *Bandwagon* 31, no. 1 (January–February 1987), 20–26.

____. "A History of the Traveling Menagerie in America, Part One." *Bandwagon* 35, no. 6 (November–December 1991), 64–71.

____. "The Out-Side Shows." *Bandwagon* 36, no. 2 (March–April 1992), 24–26.

____. "Victor Pepin's Genealogy." *Bandwagon* 36, no. 3 (May–June 1992), 31.

____. "The Yankee and the Circus." *Bandwagon* 37, no. 3 (May–June 1993), 19–25.

____. "The Circus Roots of Negro Minstrelsy." *Bandwagon* 40, no. 6 (1996), 43–45.

____. *Traveling Showmen: The American Circus before the Civil War*. Detroit: Astley & Ricketts, 1997.

____. "Parade Wagons 1847." *Bandwagon* 42, no. 2 (March–April 1998), 2–3.

____. *Annals of the American Circus*. Seattle: Dauven and Thayer, 2000.

____. *The Performers: A History of Circus Acts*. Seattle: Dauven and Thayer, 2005.

____. "The Oldest of Showmen: The Career of Benjamin F. Brown of Somers, New York." *Bandwagon* 50, no. 5 (September–October 2006), 10–16.

Thayer, Stuart, and William L. Slout. *Grand Entrée: The Birth of the Greatest Show on Earth, 1870–1875*. San Bernardino, CA: Borgo Press, 1998.

Thompson, George. *A Documentary History of the African Theatre*. Evanston, IL: Northwestern University Press, 1998.

Thomson, Rosemarie Garland, ed. *Cultural Spectacles of the Extraordinary Body*. New York: New York University Press, 1996.

Toll, Robert C. *Blacking Up: The Minstrel Show in Nineteenth Century America*. New York: Oxford University Press, 1974.

Tolles, Thayer, Lauretta Dimmick, and Donna J. Hassler, eds. *American Sculpture in the Metropolitan Museum of Art*. New York: Metropolitan Museum of Art, 1999.

Tottis, James W. *Life's Pleasures: The Ashcan Artists' Brush with Leisure, 1895–1925*. London: Merrell, 2007.

Towsen, John H. *Clowns*. New York: Hawthorne Books, 1976.

Trumble, Alfred. *A Spangled World; or, Life with the Circus*. New York: Richard K. Fox, 1883.

Vail, R. W. G. *Random Notes on the History of the Early American Circus*. Worcester, MA: American Antiquarian Society, 1934.

Valentine, D. T. *Manual of the Corporation of the City of New York for 1858*. New York: Chas. W. Baker, 1858.

Vey, Shauna. "Good Intentions and Fearsome Prejudice: New York's 1876 Act to Prevent and Punish Wrongs to Children." *Theatre Survey* 42 (2001), 53–68.

Warren, Louis S. *Buffalo Bill's America: William Cody and the Wild West Show*. New York: Alfred A. Knopf, 2005.

Watkins, Clifford E. *Showman: The Life and Music of Perry George Lowery*. Jackson: University Press of Mississippi, 2003.

"Weegee, as Clown, Covers Circus from the Inside." *PM* (July 9, 1943), 12–13.

Wemmer, Christen M., and Catherine A. Christen, eds. *Elephants and Ethics: Toward a Morality of Coexistence*. Baltimore: Johns Hopkins University Press, 2008.

White, Shane. *Somewhat More Independent: The End of Slavery in New York City, 1770–1810*. Athens: University of Georgia Press, 1991.

____. *Stories of Freedom in Black New York*. Cambridge, MA: Harvard University Press, 2002.

Wilentz, Sean. *Chants Democratic: New York City & the Rise of the American Working Class, 1788–1850*. New York: Oxford University Press, 1984.

Wittmann, Matthew. "Menageries and Markets: The Zoological Institute tours Jacksonian America." *Common-Place* 12, no. 1 (October 2011), http://www.common-place.org/vol-12/no-01/lessons/.

Wright, Richardson. *Hawkers and Walkers in Early America*. Philadelphia: J. B. Lippincott, 1927.

Photo Credits and Chronology Captions

Photographs were taken or supplied by the lending institutions, organizations, or individuals credited in the picture captions and are protected by copyright; many names are not repeated here. Individual photographers are credited below. Permission has been sought for use of all copyrighted illustrations in this volume. In several instances, despite extensive research, it has not been possible to locate the original copyright holder. Copyright owners of these works should contact the Bard Graduate Center, 18 West 86th Street, New York, NY, 10024.

(c) The Lisette Model, Foundation, Inc. (1983). Used by permission: Cat. 30

Paul Mutino: Figs. 2.7, 2.9, 2.10, 3.2; Chks. 19, 20, 29, 71, 83

Bruce White: p. 2, p. 166–167, C. 16; Figs. 1.8, 1.9, 2.1, 2.2, 2.5, 2.15, 2.16, 3.5, 3.7, Cats. 11 (lower), 16, 25B; Chks. 6, 7, 9, 34, 39, 40, 42, 52, 55, 58, 65, 86, 87, 88, 89, 90, 93, 95, 126, 214, 217

Chronology Captions

Fig. C.1 1793: *Mr. Ricketts the Equestrian Hero*, 1796. Etching. The Historical Society of Pennsylvania, Bb 96 R424.

Fig. C.2 1798: C. Milbourne. *Park Row and St. Paul's Chapel, New York*, 1798. Watercolor, brown and black ink, selective glazing, and graphite on paper. Courtesy of The New-York Historical Society, Purchase, Abbott, Belknap, Durr, and Foster-Jarvis Funds, 1953.63.

Fig. C.3 1807: "Robert Fulton's 'Clermont,' First Vessel Ever Propelled by Steam," 1807. Chromolithograph. Robert Fulton papers, Manuscripts and Archives Division, The New York Public Library, Astor, Lenox and Tilden Foundations.

Fig. C.4 1825: W. H. Bartlett. *Lockport, Erie Canal*, 1826. Engraving by William Tombleson. Print Collection, Miriam and Ira D. Wallach Division of Art, Prints and Photographs, The New York Public Library, Astor, Lenox and Tilden Foundations.

Fig. C.5 1832: *Jim Crow*, ca. 1835. Etching, published by Hodgson, 111 Fleet Street, London, and by Turner & Fisher, New York. Library of Congress, Prints and Photographs Division.

Fig. C.6 1849: "Great riot at the Astor Place opera house, New York on Thursday evening May 10th, 1849." Color lithograph, printed by Nathaniel Currier, New York. Eno Collection, Miriam and Ira D. Wallach Division of Art, Prints and Photographs, The New York Public Library, Astor, Lenox and Tilden Foundations.

Fig. C.7 1853: "Interior view of the New York Crystal Palace for the exhibition of the industry of all nations. Taken on the first of December 1853." Color lithograph by Thomas Benecke and A. Weingärtner, New York; published by Goupil & Co., New York. Eno Collection, Miriam and Ira D. Wallach Division of Art, Prints and Photographs, The New York Public Library, Astor, Lenox and Tilden Foundations.

Fig. C.8 1863: Detail of "Genl. Tom Thumb & Wife, Com. Nutt & Minnie Warren, Four Wonderously Formed & Strangely Beautiful Ladies & Gentlemen in Miniatures, Natures Smallest Editions of Her Choicest Works," 1863. Hand-colored lithograph, printed by Currier & Ives, New York. © Shelburne Museum, Shelburne, Vermont, Gift of Harry T. Peters Sr. Family, 1959, 1959-67.20. Chk. 31.

Fig. C.9 1876: Baseball game, 1888. Color lithograph, Bufford's Sons Lith. Co. Boston. Museum of the City of New York, Print Archive, 52.112.2.

Fig. C.10 1886: "Projected Statue of Liberty for New York Harbor," 1875. From *Harper's Weekly: a Journal of Civilization* (November 27, 1875), 969. Picture Collection, The New York Public Library, Astor, Lenox and Tilden Foundations.

Fig. C.11 1892: "Forepaugh & Sells Brothers Enormous Shows United. Madison Square Garden New York / The World Famous Metropolitan Home of These Combined Stupendous Shows," 1900. Poster, printed by the Strobridge Lithographing Co., Cincinnati & New York. © Shelburne Museum, Shelburne, Vermont, 1959-259.13.

Fig. C.12 1903: The Electric Towers at night, Luna Park Coney Island, N.Y., 1903. Photograph by Detroit Photographic Co. Picture Collection, The New York Public Library, Astor, Lenox and Tilden Divisions.

Fig. C.13 1912: May Wirth with horses. Signed photograph. The John and Mable Ringling Museum of Art, Tibbals Collection, ht0004443.

Fig. C.14 1927: "Contract No. 7. North tunnel—State line markers, New York—New Jersey." Holland Tunnel, 1926. Photograph. Science, Industry & Business Library, The New York Public Library, Astor, Lenox and Tilden Divisions.

Fig. C.15 1939: *Guidebook, World's Fair 1940*. New York: Rogers-Kellogg-Stillson, 1940. The Wolfsonian–Florida International University, Miami Beach, Florida, Long-term loan, The Mitchell Wolfson, Jr. Private Collection, Miami, Florida, XM1999.176.2.

Fig. C.16 1942: *Ringling Bros. Barnum & Bailey Circus Magazine*, 1942. Private collection.

Fig. C.17 1950: United Nations General Assembly Hall, ca. 1955. Postcard. Museum of the City of New York, Postcard Collection, 97.59.16.

Fig. C.18 1955: Weegee. "Whoa Nelly," 1955. Photograph. International Center of Photography / Getty Images.

Fig. C.19 1966: Lincoln Center for the Performing Arts, ca. 1965. Photograph. Museum of the City of New York, Photo Archive, X2010.11.03866.

Fig. C.20 1983: "Circus for Life, The Biggest Gay Event of All Time," 1983. Collection of The New-York Historical Society.

Fig. C.21 1974: Philippe Petit, a French high-wire artist, walks across a tightrope suspended between the World Trade Center's Twin Towers. New York, August 7, 1974. Photograph. AP Photo/Alan Welner.

Fig. C.22 2011: Barry Lubin and his clown Grandma in the Big Apple Circus, 2007. Photograph. Big Apple Circus.

Index

OPARDS.   PAIR OF KANGAROOS.   HUNTING LEOPARD.   PORCUPINE.   BENGAL TIGER.

LEOPARD.   ICHNEUMON.   SEMIA TRIBE.   PUMA.   AFRICAN PANTHER.   JACKAL

MALE ZEBRA.   BUFFALO.   THE ALPACHA.   DROMEDARY.   QUAGGA.   THE GNU

R, OR WHITE BEAR.   ROYAL TIGER, AND LIONESS.

BUFFALO.   THE ALPACHA.   DROMEDARY.   QUAGGA.   THE GNU   MALE ZEBRA.   R

AFRICAN OSTRICH.   THE EMEU.   ELEPHANT WITH SADDLE   ELEPHANT JULIET.   CA